heart & soul
INTERNET
JOB SEARCH

heart & soul

INTERNET JOB SEARCH

7 NEVER-BEFORE-PUBLISHED SECRETS
TO CAPTURING YOUR DREAM JOB
USING THE INTERNET

CHUCK COCHRAN
DONNA PEERCE

CERTIFIED PROFESSIONAL
RESUME WRITERS AND PARTNERS,
HEART & SOUL CAREER CENTER

 DAVIES-BLACK PUBLISHING • PALO ALTO, CALIFORNIA

NOTICE

*All names have been changed to protect the privacy of the individuals highlighted
in this book. Any similarities to actual persons, living or dead, are purely coincidental.*

Published by Davies-Black Publishing, an imprint of Consulting Psychologists Press, Inc.,
3803 East Bayshore Road, Palo Alto, CA 94303; 800-624-1765; www.cpp-db.com

Special discounts on bulk quantities of Davies-Black books are available to corporations, professional associations, and other organizations. For details, contact the Director of Book Sales at Davies-Black Publishing, an imprint of Consulting Psychologists Press, Inc., 3803 East Bayshore Road, Palo Alto, CA 94303; 650-691-9123; Fax 650-988-0673.

Cover and interior design by Seventeenth Street Studios

03 02 01 00 99   10 9 8 7 6 5 4 3 2 1
Printed in the United States of America

Library of Congress Cataloging-in-Publication Data
Cochran, Chuck
    Heart & soul internet job search : 7 never-before-published secrets to capturing
    your dream job using the Internet / Chuck Cochran, Donna Peerce.
       p.   cm.
    Includes index.
    ISBN 0-89106-125-8
    1. Job hunting—Computer network resources. 2. Internet (Computer network).
    3. Résumés (Employment)—Computer networks. I. Peerce, Donna. II. Title.
    III. Title: Heart and soul Internet job search.
  HF5382.7.C6   1999
  025.06′65014—dc21   98-51049
                                            CIP

FIRST EDITION
First printing 1999

Contents

Preface

This is not your typical "Internet job search" book. It won't bombard you with page after page of technical jargon and leave you overwhelmed and exasperated. It won't take you on endless, taxing searches that leave you confused and aggravated. What it will do is take you to new heights in learning about yourself while finding that dream job you've been passionate about for so long—but never knew how to find. Inside are seven secrets to knowing and believing in yourself that will help you make your Internet job search productive and successful. You'll learn how to put heart and soul into your dreams and goals. This book is for entry-level job seekers as well as for seasoned professionals who want a job that speaks to them on a heart and soul level.

Most people don't think of heart and soul when they think of an Internet job search, but really, nothing could be more appropriate. If you want to do anything right, then you must put heart and soul into it. They are involved in everything we do in life. If they aren't, then it simply isn't worth doing. Heart and soul are the crux of our existence. The two form a synergy that is the very breath of life.

Heart and soul are important aspects of our lives, even on the Internet. If you don't know who you are and are not focused in your life, the Internet can confuse you even more. Because the Internet contains an enormous amount of information, you must be extremely focused in your career and job search to get the most out of the World Wide Web. People make the mistake of aimlessly surfing the Web, hoping to find a great job, without ever developing an idea or concept of what they want to do in their life and career. They do this without stopping to search their inner selves—their heart and soul—or learning how to effectively use the Internet to their advantage.

If you want to accomplish anything, you must create a vision of your success and then build a solid life plan to achieve this vision. To make your next career move a great one, rather than just average, you need to embrace the concepts discussed here in *Heart & Soul Internet Job Search*. This book is for individuals who want a job they'll love—one that matches their heart's dreams. It's for those professionals who are looking for a higher-caliber career that suits them emotionally, physically, and spiritually. The seven secrets can help you take advantage of the Internet to find a perfect job. Many of you, we know, are already experienced or at least knowledgeable Internet users, so we have avoided the elementary phases of getting on and using the Internet (we have, however, included a "Getting Wired" section, as Appendix I, for beginners). In this book, we focus on how to harness and control the Internet with regard to your mission, dreams, goals, and daily life plan!

You'll find that the Internet offers fantastic career opportunities for those who know how to utilize this resource effectively. We will show you how to control and disseminate the vast amount of information that is available to you and how to utilize your vision in your search. Armed with a strong vision and the knowledge of our seven secrets, your use of the Internet will take on new meaning. With proper focus, the broad scope of the Internet narrows to a manageable subset. All of a sudden this enormous store of information on the

Internet becomes a personal library of specific resources and job opportunities that are tailored and relevant only to you!

So whether you're an Internet genius or a computer novice, the information you really need to know is in this book. Rather than bombarding you with hundreds of Web sites that you need to visit and boring you with lengthy, laborious details of the Internet (which change daily), we show you how to make the Internet work for you in a simple, easy-to-read style that's interesting, fun, and thought-provoking. We've illustrated an easy but more in-depth way to incorporate the Heart & Soul approach when using the Internet and outlined them in these seven secrets.

After thorough research, study, and experience, we know what sorts of Internet job search techniques work and which don't. Conducting an Internet job search alone can be quite intimidating, if not boring, overwhelming, and tedious. This book is a reliable resource that shows you where to go and how to use the Net to your advantage!

Imagine all the businesses that are on the Net right now. Think of the millions and millions of different companies' sites that you could visit. The Internet consists of thousands of connected networks around the world, and these networks consist of numerous companies, government agencies, and organizations. To be effective and successful in using the Internet in your job search, you must know how to organize, disseminate, and control the information to help you find exactly what you want. This is getting to the real heart and soul of the Internet job search, and this is what we explain in this book.

Employers use the Internet in the way that suits them best. Not every company recruits in the same manner, and not every hiring manager or human resource department uses the Internet in the same way. But you will soon learn the definitive way to get hired using the Internet as we show you the *Seven Never-Before-Published Secrets to Capturing Your Dream Job.*

The *Heart & Soul Internet Job Search* is the second book in our *Heart & Soul* series, and it stands independent from our first book, *Heart & Soul Resumes.* Even though we would love for you to read all our books in the Heart & Soul series, it is certainly not necessary. Our books work independently, as well as complementarily, to build a holistic, creative synergy that's designed to help you find the job you'll love and become the best that you can be, personally, physically, spiritually, and professionally.

We invite you to join us in our Heart & Soul adventure!

—Chuck Cochran and Donna Peerce

HEART & SOUL TIP

Even though they have subtly different meanings, we will use the words Internet, Net, Information Superhighway, cyberspace, Web, and World Wide Web interchangeably. For our purposes, they are all practically the same thing.

1 Looking Behind the Screens at How Employers Use the Internet

Even if you are on the right track, you'll get run over if you just sit there.

WILL ROGERS

WHAT BETTER WAY TO whet your appetite for a Heart & Soul Internet job search than to hear from the people who are hiring on-line right now? We have interviewed many professional hiring managers to learn how they incorporate the Internet into their recruiting efforts. In this chapter, we explore the first of the seven never-before-published secrets to capturing your dream job using the Internet—going behind those computer screens to learn how employers use the Internet to find you.

Making a Heart & Soul Connection on the Internet

With all the commotion and hype about the plenitude of positions being filled through the Internet, you may wonder how employment matches really are being made in cyberspace. With each passing year, the employers we interview have seen a dramatic increase in their on-line recruiting efforts. Nobody doubts the enormous impact the Internet is having and will continue to have on the employment industry. Regarding your Internet job search, you must know how people are getting hired on-line now and what trends you can expect to develop in the future.

How Do Employers Find Candidates?

Simply put, employers categorize candidates who contact them in two ways: solicited and unsolicited. Although many consistently hire people who send their resumes unsolicited and/or who attempt to network with them, most employers agree that they put the majority of their energy and effort into those high-caliber candidates who respond to job postings they have advertised, often on-line. Remember this when you plan your job search. You not only want to aggressively research and respond to job postings (on-line and off), but you also want to target employers on your own, whether you know they are hiring or not. We'll explore this in much more detail later, but for now, let's look at how employers recruit on-line.

When employers need a candidate, they advertise through whatever media elicit the best response. The Internet is an extremely cost-effective way to recruit as long as the employer posts job openings in a popular, well-visited Web site (this may be their own Web site). Right now, employers are testing and retesting their recruiting ads to find out how they can find the best people for the smallest amount of money. While traditional forms of advertising such as newspapers and trade journals are well established and very predictable, the Internet offers the most potential now and in the future.

Different companies are successful on the Internet in different ways. For example, if the company has a good reputation and is of at least moderate size, it often gets excellent responses by advertising for positions on its own Web site. People often search the company's Web site for information on job openings. However, if the company is new or small, or has yet to develop a reputation or name recognition, no one will know how to reach the site in the first place. For these companies, third-party resume/job opportunity databases offer the greatest exposure. These database sites are Web sites that maintain a host of active job seekers' resumes and current job openings in any number of industries, located anywhere in the world. Because the Internet is a relatively new resource, however, no employer counts on only one method of on-line recruiting. They are all trying several kinds of on-line advertising and tracking their successes respectively.

Many employers also utilize newsgroups, e-mail mailing lists, and even chat rooms on the Internet to recruit for top employees. Employers are aggressively using the Internet to find employees, and you need to be equally as aggressive in making yourself available. Keep in mind that headhunters and employment agencies also search for good candidates on-line. The Internet is an ideal place to make connections, and that is where you need to be.

Meredith Clayton, Executive Recruiter

Meredith Clayton is a successful executive recruiter who has worked hard to get where she is today. She specializes in technological industries and earns excellent money finding jobs for technical-oriented people. She and her husband are planning on sending their children to college and retiring in the Caribbean. Their future didn't always look so bright, however. Meredith recalled the difficult times she had in her first year as a recruiter. Money was so tight that they couldn't even save a penny. But Meredith persevered and, using the Internet to her advantage, began to close some big deals and place candidates in outstanding jobs.

Traditionally, recruiters have always made their living on the telephone, and most still do. They place numerous phone calls to find job orders from employers, to find and screen candidates, and to follow up on the interviews. In fact, the best recruiters average four hours on the phone each day. However, with the growing use of the Internet, this practice may change forever.

When Meredith started working as a recruiter, she had a difficult time, especially with the phone. She tried to fit into the company's mold of top recruiter, but she just couldn't make it happen. Every time she looked at the phone, her stomach started turning into knots—she just hated the intense phone work required in her job. But she stuck with it. She knew that eventually she would find a way to put her strengths and talents to work for her. After all, she really did want to help people find jobs.

Being fairly computer literate, Meredith felt that she could utilize the Internet to her advantage. She viewed the Internet as an opportunity that many recruiters had overlooked. She knew that more and more people, especially technology-related job seekers and employers, were using the

Internet for recruiting. Unfortunately, her boss was from the "old school" and demanded that she use the telephone during peak business hours. She grudgingly obliged. Days turned into weeks, and weeks into months, and she wasn't even close to a deal. "Don't worry," they told her. "Sometimes it takes six months to a year to get your first big placement."

But she didn't want to wait another six months; she wanted success immediately. So one night, when she was all alone in the office, she logged on to the

Internet. She didn't expect immediate results, but she decided she could at least learn more about the Internet. After 15 minutes of surfing the Web, she located a career Web site that referenced all the other major career Web sites. This was exciting! Night after night, Meredith logged on to the best career sites to review the new job postings and resumes in technology. She researched new sites as well. After a week or two, she began to feel confident about what kinds of information she could access and how she might be able to use this information to her advantage.

One night, while searching for something unrelated, she found a job opening that was posted by a company she had been trying to solicit a job order from for the last three months. She also found five candidates from other sites that might be a good match for the job posting. Her heart began to pound as she considered that she could place one of these candidates with this company and finally earn a good commission check.

In the past, whenever Meredith had telephoned this particular company they politely took her call but dismissed her solicitation for a job order. The day after she found the job posting, she called the employer and mentioned that she had found some excellent candidates for the job advertised on the Internet. This time, the company was much more receptive because they had tried to fill that spot for several months and were in dire need of a qualified candidate. They agreed to interview Meredith's candidates for this position.

Immediately after speaking to the employer, she began to call and screen the people she had found on the Internet. She also screened several other candidates from her personal database. Since she wanted to make an outstanding impression with this employer, she was careful not to refer anyone who wasn't highly qualified for the job. She set up interviews for three of her best choices—two from her database and one from the Internet. By the end of the week, the Internet candidate had completed five interviews with all the major decision makers of the company. The job was offered and accepted that week. Meredith's first sizable commission check came the very next week, and Meredith was elated with how the Internet had helped her.

HEART & SOUL TIP

Recruiters do find jobs on the Internet. Utilizing this approach to finding jobs will make an impact on your Heart & Soul Internet job search.

Dumbfounded by and curious about her surge of productive activity, Meredith's boss asked her how she had managed to score such an important assignment. To his amazement and chagrin, Meredith showed him step-by-step how the Internet had helped her produce this particular deal. Meredith pointed out that her telephone skills were critical, but it was the Internet that had led her to both the employer and the candidate.

Her boss wasn't much for saying he was wrong, but in the next weekly meeting he announced to his entire staff of recruiters that they would now be incorporating the Internet into their marketing efforts. "From now on," he demanded, "everyone must spend at least two hours a week recruiting on the Internet!"

HEART & SOUL TIP

Post your resume in as many reputable career-related Web sites as possible because you never know who is looking! Recruiters, employers, colleagues, and anyone who might be able to help or refer you could come across your resume.

Despite such success stories, some recruiters are hesitant to use the Internet because they use a system that has worked for them for years. But be assured that you can expect more and more recruiters to expand their on-line searching efforts for their candidates. The lesson for the job seeker is to post your resume in as many reputable places as possible because you never know who is looking.

Companies, for the most part, try to be as objective and fair in their hiring as possible, but the bottom line is that you get hired when you make a personal connection with the decision maker—in other words, when you make a Heart & Soul connection. Granted, this decision maker might simply be intrigued with your experience and past accomplishments, but somehow the decision maker thinks that you may be able to solve the company's problems or make them more money.

We'll Keep Your Resume on File

"We'll keep your resume on file," used to be the kiss of death. Hearing that meant your resume would either be thrown away or lost forever in some manila folder in an archaic filing system. That's what it used to be like, by no fault of the employer, though; although they might have tried to keep you "alive" in their system of applicants, with the volume of resumes they received on a daily basis, the old manual system was unfair and expensive to maintain.

Traditionally, the recruiting side of a human resource (HR) department has been very labor intensive. As people would apply or send in resumes, HR would catalogue each resume and file it away in some large filing cabinet. Whenever HR wanted to hire a new employee, they would go back to the big cabinet and pull out all the relevant resumes and start calling all the "potentials" to set up interviews. This process alone doesn't seem that complex, but when you consider that some employers get 50 to 100 or even 1,000 resumes a day, the paperwork can be astounding. Not only is this expensive, but it is also imperfect and inefficient. Resumes get lost, they get filed in the wrong place, and too many things go wrong. So when a few innovative technological companies developed a computerized scanning system that would eliminate all the filing and paper shuffling, many employers followed suit.

The idea is simple. When a resume comes in, it's put in a computerized scanner. The scanner reads each word and places it in a specific file. The physical resume is thrown away. For example, when an accounting department needs a certified public accountant with tax and cost accounting experience, they ask the computer to generate resumes for that position. The computer searches its files for keywords like *accountant, tax,* and *cost accounting.* The resumes that contain these words used several times throughout will be considered "strong" matches. This type of system efficiently reduces the labor involved in managing new hires and also screens candidates with fair, objective criteria. A computer can't be biased regarding sex, color, age, race, or religion, relieving the employer of some legal liability exposure as well.

Later, in Chapter 3, we demonstrate how to convert your Heart & Soul resume to a scannable resume using key words. This is very important to know because, if you submit a resume for a job opening and don't get an offer, or if you send a resume unsolicited, most employers will still keep your resume in their system for future job openings. If you have submitted your resume correctly, you will be considered for other job openings.

Why Are Companies "Net Hiring"?

Due to the expense, recruiting systems and recruiting automation was limited for a long time. Only a few major companies could afford the expensive scanning and in-house applicant management systems. The Internet, however, offers employers the same efficiency as the scanning systems, and using the Internet can be potentially much less expensive while at least as productive.

HEART & SOUL TIP

The Internet offers employers the same efficiency as expensive scanning systems and is potentially much less expensive and just as productive.

HEART & SOUL TIP

Recruiting on the Internet is cost-effective and a good strategy for the employer. What once took a large human resource staff to manage now takes only a few computer technicians to update and maintain the company's data-base of job openings and resumes.

When you log on to the Internet and visit a company's Web site, you actually share the expense of the employer's system. Your own computer and your Internet access are paid for by you. The employer simply interfaces the company's internal computer to the Internet so you can successfully transfer your resume or read about new job opportunities.

For a fraction of the cost, a modest investment in the Internet and an information management system can produce a sophisticated system equivalent to any stand-alone in-house applicant tracking system. To the small company, the Internet offers a way to compete with the big employers; to the large company, the Internet offers a way to supplement its existing systems and closely interact with applicants.

Dean Witherspoon, Human Resource Manager

Dean's job is to recruit people for his employer. He works for a manufacturer of injection-molded parts that are used in a variety of industries and products. His company is growing at a rate of 20 percent a year and is hiring new people at the same pace. Department managers are not allowed to screen or initially interview for positions they need to fill. All prospective employees must meet with Dean or one of his staff before being sent to any of the department managers for more in-depth interviews. The system is cumbersome, but it assures fair and equal management of all prospective employees and new hires.

Generally, the way it works is that any manager with a certain level of authority in the company will complete a job order and submit it to Dean. Dean sends that manager three to ten qualified candidates to interview. Dean ensures that each new applicant meets minimum company standards as well as specific standards that the manager has determined are necessary for the job in question. If the manager specifically requests an interview with a certain candidate, Dean will make sure that the person is included in the interview process.

When Dean took this position, his job was to streamline the HR department and overhaul the recruiting process by using the Internet. He wasn't very technically adept and almost didn't take the job because he was sure it would be a difficult chore. But the job offered a good salary, and he knew he'd have to jump on the technology bandwagon sooner or later or he was going to be left behind.

Dean's most difficult obstacle in converting HR to an Internet-savvy department was the fact that he was going to have to terminate ten HR administrative employees. The company agreed that Dean could offer transfers to all but one employee, who decided to quit anyway.

Dean's first hiring challenge was recruiting a couple of computer information technicians and Internet wizards. After negotiating their salaries, Dean thought he might very well be in the wrong career because he saw how difficult it was to recruit good talent in the competitive field of technology.

He and his Internet team decided that accepting paper and text-based resumes would be the best way to manage resumes and applicants. They decided to require that all candidates submit their resumes in a text file first, either attached to an e-mail or via the company Web site. If an applicant didn't have access to the company's site or the Internet, a paper resume, preferably on disk in a text file, could be submitted. The upside to this system is that text-file resumes are easily managed and don't require purchases of expensive systems (relatively speaking). The downside came when applicants submitted their resumes only on paper. This problem, they decided, was not insurmountable because the employees in production were not required to submit a resume at all and management candidates who didn't send resumes in text files could be scanned into the system without much additional cost.

HEART & SOUL TIP

It's very effective to submit your resume in both the standard paper (presentation) format and in the electronic, text-based, scannable resume so that employers can scan these text-based resumes into their databases.

After a difficult 18-month transition, the company has come to love Dean's new recruiting system. Resumes that enter the system are automatically entered into the database for future use. When Dean gets a job order, he pulls up the most qualified applicants from the new company database and calls them in for a screening and subsequent interviews with the appropriate department heads.

To supplement his in-house database, Dean also advertises for "open" jobs in the newspaper and on a major career Web site. Dean says even he was a little surprised at how much money the new system saved the company. He claims the system paid for itself in less than six months!

How April Parker Hired John Anderson Using the Internet

Another HR manager, April Parker, works for one of the largest toy manufacturing companies in the world, based in New York City. It's her responsibility to locate and recruit top-notch computer specialists and designers to build CD-ROM games for the company's technological division. While many great candidates in computer technology are available, not all of them have the vision and creativity necessary to create games.

In addition to those skills, April needed someone who had management, personnel, and budget experience because this new employee would have to head up a whole department. She knew it was going to be difficult to find a person with all these skills.

April had been trying to find a creative CD-ROM game designer for several months. She had contacted several headhunters, posted the position on the company Web page and with two major Internet resume databases networked with other companies, and placed ads in trade magazines and in the newspaper. As you might expect, her Internet recruiting efforts paid off far more than the "traditional" methods.

HEART & SOUL TIP

It's easy to be positive and up-beat in life when things are going well. However, the real test comes when you are challenged. This is the time that your true character can shine through.

Meanwhile, John Anderson telephoned us from Santa Monica, California. A friend of his had referred him to us and suggested that perhaps we could help. John, a computer whiz, had been out of work for three months and was getting desperate. "I know I'm supposed to be positive about this job search thing," John explained. "I know that if I become negative, then I'm going to draw negative experiences to me. But right now, all I'm worried about is how I'm going to pay the mortgage."

We told John that we certainly understood his predicament. It's easy to be positive and upbeat when life is going well, but when it gets tough, your character and strength must pull you through. Of course, when you don't know how you're going to pay the mortgage, it's understandable that you're going to have some tense, anxious moments of self-doubt.

We asked John what he had been doing to find work. John's answer was the usual, "Well, I've been looking in trade magazines and newspapers, but it doesn't seem like there's anything available for me. I'm overqualified for most positions. And, of course, I've been cruising the Internet, but I haven't found anything very interesting."

We explained that he needed to focus on what he really wanted to do instead of aimlessly surfing the Web. He was so talented and diverse in his computer and technology skills that he had actually lost his focus on what he truly wanted. We asked John to describe what he loved the most, what he felt passionate about. He needed to define what his heart and soul needed.

After a couple weeks of career coaching and ongoing conversations, John admitted that he really wanted to design and build CD-ROM games for a major toy company, but he wasn't sure how to locate and obtain work with this kind of company. We explained that we could rewrite his resume and help him search for toy companies on the Internet. We also explained that, in order to be proactive, he needed to approach the companies of his choice and offer them a proposal. He had thought, like many people, that if a company doesn't have an opening and isn't actively advertising, then why bother sending a resume? More than likely, his type of job wouldn't be advertised widely anyway. He didn't realize that many jobs are actually created for people who have outstanding backgrounds; it was possible that he could approach a company that had no job openings and the company would create one just for him.

HEART & SOUL TIP

It's important to actively submit resumes to companies that you'd like to work for whether they have job openings or not, instead of just sending them to companies that advertise job openings.

Now that John had identified a plan and mission, we were able to rewrite his resume with more focus—which is always more successful than a general resume. We decided that he should have two styles of resume: a traditional one and an electronic version for the Internet. Following are the resume (Figure 1.1) we prepared for him from the notes gleaned from our interviews, a supplementary one-page bio (Figure 1.2), and a cover letter (Figure 1.3). We also prepared an electronic version of his resume so he could submit it on the Internet. (We'll show you how to convert your resume for the Internet in Chapter 3.)

After John received this resume and the electronic version for the Internet, we set him loose. He was already a natural on the Internet! Now that he had a genuine focus and vision, his job search took on a whole new meaning. He diligently and specifically searched only for major toy manufacturers. Within the first 45 minutes of being on the Internet, he told us that he had found one of April Parker's job listings. He e-mailed her his resume and then mailed her a presentation brochure. (We always recommend following up with a hard copy of your resume in the mail if you have the address. A hard copy makes a more dynamic presentation.)

HEART & SOUL TIP

People are finding their dream jobs every day on the Internet!

This was a match made in heaven! April contacted John immediately, and after a couple of on-line interviews the hiring company flew him out to their home office. That same day, they offered John a job, one that he had been dreaming of. And John didn't even have to move—he could work out of his home in California!

John's story isn't a unique one. People are finding their dream jobs every day on the Internet. All it takes is vision, focus, researching of target companies, and a great resume. You, too, can have success like this!

FIGURE 1.1
John Anderson's Brochure Resume (Cover Sheet)

HEART & SOUL TIP

We designed a brochure portfolio type of resume for John to showcase his experience and qualifications. This resume is actually three pages long, but it can be formatted to fit in a brochure.

JOHN ANDERSON

A Presentation
of
Professional Credentials
in Computer Animation, Training, and Management

123 Anywhere Street
City, State 10000
Phone Number
john@saltwater.com

■ **FIGURE 1.1 CONTINUED**
John Anderson's Brochure Resume (Page 1)

HEART & SOUL TIP

John's Professional Profile sums up his qualifications and goals. This is the first thing an employer will read.

JOHN ANDERSON

123 Anywhere Street
City, State 10000
Phone Number
john@saltwater.com

Professional Profile

Multitalented, creative, experienced Director of Animation & Director of Training with more than 18 years of comprehensive experience in animation, training, management, and production. Strong general management qualifications with talents in planning and spearheading the development and implementation of animation departments and training programs. In-depth experience in teaching numerous classes, including production, lighting & lenses, UNIX, NT, Wavefront, SoftImage, Prisms, Elastic Reality, Motion Capture, and UNIX for animators in production. Comprehensive background in developing scenes for CD-ROM games and programs.

Extensive background working with producers and directors to analyze and define computer graphics, software, and hardware needs. Create a team-oriented management structure and utilize a participative decision-making management style in solving problems. Adept at analyzing whole picture, identifying problems, and resolving issues. Ability to build and nurture client relationships in hectic, fast-paced, tense environments. International expertise in working with directors and producers abroad.

Creative visionary who desires a leadership position with a major toy manufacturer that will provide a challenging avenue for career growth and development in the world of animation, training, and production.

EDUCATION

Bachelor of Arts in Architecture & Computer Design
Southern California Institute, 1980
University of Southern California Film School, 1972

Certifications & Computer Animation & Systems

- Certified SoftImage L3 & Wavefront Master Instructor
- C-Shell scripting, HTML scripts, VRML, UNIX, Mac, DOS, Windows, AMIGA-DOS, Wavefront & SoftImage, Alias & Prisms, R&H Custom Modeler, PC & AMIGA software, Word, Excel, Access, PhotoShop, and general PC programs

Project Management Highlights

- *Company Development:* Held full responsibility for planning, developing, and initiating a complete 3-D training facility. This involved capital equipment acquisition, recruiting and staffing personnel, budget management, and building and nurturing of client/owner relationships.

- *Recording Studio & Edit Bay Development:* Responsible for designing, building, and wiring video recording studio & edit bay for SCI-ARC.
- *Presentation System Development:* Managed the development and production of a usable CD-ROM–based "laptop" courtroom presentation system for lawyers.
- *Mental Images Demo Reel Creation:* Implemented the creation of a four-minute animation demo reel for the company, which was accepted into the juried COMPUTERGRAPHICS Electronic Theater program.

Freelance Animation & Computer Graphics Experience

Freelance Animator

- *CD-ROM Games:* On a freelance basis, created and designed scenes for CD-ROM games including the following: Casino lobby scene for "InterWorld Casino," an Internet CD-ROM game; the Introductory scene for "Conquest & Reign," on CD-ROM; and the Cove City, town and cave scenes for "Drako's Island," an Internet-based World.

Freelance Computer Graphics Consultant

- *Consultant:* Provided on-site consulting services on a freelance basis for a variety of clients. Reviewed and analyzed production departments to identify problems. Integrated systems and reengineered production methods to streamline operations and increase efficiency.
- *Clientele:* Major clientele has included: McDonnell-Douglas, Rhythm & Hues, Topix, MetroLight, Novocom, and Lockheed.

Professional Management & Training Experience

Director of Training
MEDIA INSTITUTE, Hollywood, California, 1995 to 1997

- *Training:* Responsible for developing and facilitating a "Train-the-Trainer Program" for SoftImage. Developed tutorials for advanced classes. Taught Production, Lighting & Lenses, UNIX, NT, and Executive Overview classes.
- *Client Relations:* Responsible for developing, building, and nurturing client relationships with software manufacturers.
- *Troubleshooter:* Reviewed and identified problems within systems and employee relations. Utilized creative problem-solving techniques to resolve issues.

Director
FXXX, INC., Hollywood, California, 1994 to 1995

- *Animation Education Department Development:* Created and established an educational facility and program to teach high-end animation software and production techniques to Hollywood entertainment industry clients. Taught classes in Wavefront, SoftImage, Prisms, Elastic Reality, Motion Capture, and UNIX for animators in production. Interviewed, hired, trained, and supervised staff and teachers.

Director of Animation Services & Chair of ALPS Software Development
ADI GRAPHICS COMPANY, Los Angeles, California, 1991 to 1994

- *Company Track Record of Success:* Began with ADI as a system administrator and lead animator and advanced to Director of Animation Services in 1993. In 1994, was also given the responsibility of chairing the ALPS Software Development Committee as a result of outstanding job performance.

■ **FIGURE 3.5**
Evelyn Blythe's Scannable Resume (Page 1)

EVELYN Q. BLYTHE
1111 Anywhere Street
City, State 10000
www.internetprovider.com/~blythe
Phone Number

EXECUTIVE PROFILE
High-caliber, successful Banking Executive with more than 24 years of experience building and leading integrated operations within a large national banking institution, servicing both commercial and retail business markets. Promoted rapidly through a series of increasingly responsible positions to final assignment as Senior Vice President of American First Bank. Introduced innovative lending, real estate financing, commercial banking, and operating policies/procedures that positively impacted revenue, profit, and portfolio growth. Appointed to several high-profile committees including Diversity Planning Council Member.

Strong general management qualifications in business analysis and operations, financial market analysis, organizational reengineering, budget management, marketing, and all facets of quality, process, and quality improvement. Excellent background in employee development, training, and leadership. Outstanding analytical, planning, organization, and negotiation skills.

Desire a position in leadership and management that will provide a challenging opportunity to significantly contribute to a company's efficiency, organization, growth, and profitability.

EDUCATION
Graduate Diploma in Banking
GRADUATE SCHOOL OF BANKING
UNIVERSITY OF NEW YORK, New York, New York

Associate of Science in Banking
STATE TECHNICAL INSTITUTE, New York, New York

Basic, Standard, General & Advanced Certificates
AMERICAN INSTITUTE OF BANKING

National Commercial Lending School
UNIVERSITY OF COLORADO, Boulder, Colorado

Diploma in Banking
NEW YORK BANKERS SCHOOL
STERN UNIVERSITY, New York, New York

Bachelor of Science in Business Administration
COLORADO STATE UNIVERSITY, Fort Collins, CO

ADVANCED TRAINING & DEVELOPMENT
Radar Training, American First Bank
RPM Training, American First Bank
Leadership NOW, American First Bank
Teambuilding, American First Bank
LEAP & Appraisals, American First Bank
Diversity, American First Bank

■ **FIGURE 3.5 CONTINUED**
Evelyn Blythe's Scannable Resume (Page 2)

EXECUTIVE BANKING EXPERIENCE

Senior Vice President
CREDIT REVIEW DIVISION - AMERICAN FIRST BANK, New York, New York - 1973 to Present
Company Track Record of Success: Began with bank in 1973 as a Commercial Loan Officer, and consistently advanced to positions of higher levels of responsibility and authority due to outstanding job performance and strong commitment to success. Positions have included Regional Commercial Loan Manager (1980 to 1987), Branch Manager for Special Assets Bank (1987 to 1992), CRO & Private Client Specialist (1992 to 1995), State Manager of Tennessee Credit Review (1995 to 1996), and current position as Senior Vice President.

Senior Vice President: Hold full responsibility for the operations of the banking institution. Responsible for examining and analyzing commercial lending units and commercial portfolios. In charge of reviewing and approving the underwriting documents to ensure they conform to corporate lending policies. Analyze and advise on credit originating in commercial lending units.

Public Speaking: Facilitate numerous meetings and seminars and speak publicly concerning banking practices, rules, regulations, and methods.

Committees & Special Projects: Appointed to several high-profile committees including Diversity Planning Council Member, Business Advisor for INROADS corporate interns, AUV Task Force, Policies & Procedures Task Force, and Associate Incentive Plan Administration.

Company Reengineering: Selected as a member of the Reengineering Project Team for the Private Client Group. As part of senior management group, responsible for restructuring and reengineering management practices for this Private Client Group, which streamlined operations and increased efficiency.

Manager of New York Credit Review: Managed and directed overall credit review. Assisted in developing and writing the bank's comprehensive lending and credit policies and procedures for American First Bank.

Personnel & Supervision: Interviewed, hired, trained, and supervised Credit Review Officers, Relationship Managers, Special Asset Officers, and Administrative Assistants. Delegated work responsibilities and monitored overall job performances to ensure accuracy and adherence to specifications, standards, rules, and regulations.

Budget Management: Review, analyze, and administer budget for operating expenditures. Review monthly and year-end financial reports and analyze budget variances. Initiate appropriate strategies to more aggressively control expenditures and changes in organizational structures.

Branch Manager for Special Assets Bank: Held full responsibility for managing overall branch operations and for collections of problem and delinquent accounts.

Portfolio Management: Reviewed and monitored loan portfolios, serving as Examiner In Charge (EIC) or Credit Review Officer (CRO) for various exams in and out of State of New York. Held full responsibility and decision-making authority for establishing and ensuring corporate policy. Led a team of officers and managed portfolio consisting of manufacturing, agricultural, professional, executive, wholesale, and retail loans.

References Available Upon Request

■ **FIGURE 3.6**
Evelyn Blythe's Cover Letter for Scannable Resume

EVELYN Q. BLYTHE
1111 Anywhere Street
City, State 10000
www.internetprovider.com/~blythe
Phone Number

Are you looking for a highly motivated, goal-oriented Executive to become a leader in your organization? I am confident that, with my experience, training, and commitment to success, I can significantly contribute to your company's team of professionals. For your review, I have enclosed a personal resume that provides details concerning my background and credentials.

As you will note in my resume, I am not a beginner but rather a seasoned professional with more than 24 years of experience building and leading integrated operations within a large national banking institution. My areas of expertise and qualifications include the following:

Proven track record of success in all facets of management, negotiations, corporate policy development, and financial analysis.

In-depth experience in examining and analyzing commercial lending units and commercial portfolios. Led a team of officers and managed portfolio consisting of manufacturing, agricultural, professional, executive, wholesale, and retail loans.

Have served as Examiner in Charge (EIC) and Credit Review Officer (CRO) for various exams in and out of state of New York.

Successfully managed and administered multimillion-dollar budgets and initiated appropriate strategies to aggressively control expenditures.

Proactive leader with effective team-building skills. Empower associates to think and work independently and in a team environment, which increases employee morale, productivity, and efficiency.

Proven ability to define issues, propose solutions, and implement changes.

I sincerely believe that, with my experience and career aspirations, I would be an asset to your organization. I would appreciate an opportunity to meet with you to discuss your upcoming plans and long-term goals, along with how my leadership and management abilities could be instrumental in achieving success for your company.

Thank you in advance for your time and consideration. I look forward to speaking with you soon.

Sincerely,

Evelyn Q. Blythe

Understanding Key Words for Your Scannable Resume

Key words are descriptive nouns and key phrases. Even though we usually preach the use of good active verbs (and still do), your scannable resume must also use descriptive nouns, such as "Cost Accountant," "Network Administrator," or "District Sales Manager."

Table 3.2 lists a few examples of key words for which a resume scanning system might search. Remember, the computer will be looking for words that are related to the position for which you're applying. You want to use as many key words as possible throughout your resume. The examples in Table 3.2 are key words for which the computer might search if you were applying for a programming/computer analyst position in a health care environment. Use Worksheet 3.1 to list all the key words you can think of that relate to you and your career.

HEART & SOUL TIP

Use as many key words as possible when you prepare your scannable resume.

Computer Programmer	Computer Analyst
C++, UNIX, Cobol, Windows NT	Network Administrator
Systems Designer	Hospital
Health Care	Medical
Multimedia Designer	Systems/Software Engineers
Database Administration	Mainframe Development
Client Server Development	Practice Management Software
Applications Developer	Intranet Administrator
Computer Operator	Systems Analyst
Programmer Analyst	Maintaining Database Archives
UNIX System Administration	UNIX Sun Solaris
Microsoft Product Specialist	Client/Server Specialist
Internet Developer	AS/400 Programmer/Analyst
Computer Installation	Computer Troubleshooting
Applications Developer	Relational Database Specialists

■ **TABLE 3.2**
Sample Key Words for a Programming/Computer Analyst Position

KEY WORDS

List all the descriptive nouns and phrases you can think of that relate to you and your career. Make sure all these key words are interwoven into your resume so that the computer can select yours in the scanning process!

■ **WORKSHEET 3.1**
List Your Own Key Words

Key Words Exercise: Test Your Use of Key Words

To make sure your newly converted resume has a good mix of key words, try the following exercise. Make a physical copy of your newly converted resume. With a highlighter, mark all the descriptive nouns and phrases (key words) in your resume. Notice that Evelyn Blythe's converted scannable resume (see Figure 3.7) and cover letter (see Figure 3.8 on page 65) have implemented a variety of key words.

After you complete this visual exercise, if you don't see enough key words or a good mix of key words, rework your resume and make the appropriate changes.

Using E-mail in Your Job Search

This is an exciting step for you—sending your resume via the Internet. This is the most fundamental step in making a Heart & Soul connection on-line. While e-mail is probably the main reason any of us gets on-line in the first place, the Internet's plethora of information and resources does a great job of keeping us there.

Throughout your job searching and networking, you will use e-mail often. Sometimes you will be sending only a brief message; other times you may need to send a complete proposal or resume. Just as often, you will be receiving and replying to similar messages. Make sure you have a thorough understanding of your e-mail before you continue. Your Internet service provider (ISP) should provide all the help and resources you need to get up and running on their e-mail software. Table 3.3 on page 66 contains a number of exercises to help you become familiar with e-mail tasks.

Attaching Resume Documents to Your E-mail

For most people, the process of attaching and sending a document via e-mail is simple. Usually you use a menu command that says "Attach Document" or an icon that looks like a paper clip to do the job. After you select the command or button, you are instructed to find the document you want to attach from your computer's directory structure. Click on the document and a copy of the document is attached to your e-mail. When you send that e-mail, a copy of the document will be sent as an attachment. These few steps might feel a little bit cumbersome if you've never done them before, but after a few tries, it will become easy.

One potential problem with attaching documents can occur if the receiver does not have the exact version of software you used to write the document. Even though many programs have excellent conversion utilities, invariably

■ FIGURE 3.7
Evelyn Blythe's Scannable Resume with Key Words Highlighted (Page 1)

EVELYN Q. BLYTHE
1111 Anywhere Street
City, State 10000
www.internetprovider.com/~blythe
Phone Number

EXECUTIVE PROFILE
High-caliber, successful Banking Executive with more than 24 years of experience building and leading integrated operations within a large national banking institution, servicing both commercial and retail business markets. Promoted rapidly through a series of increasingly responsible positions to final assignment as Senior Vice President of American First Bank. Introduced innovative lending, real estate financing, commercial banking, and operating policies/procedures that positively impacted revenue, profit, and portfolio growth. Appointed to several high-profile committees including Diversity Planning Council Member .

Strong general management qualifications in business analysis and operations, financial market analysis, organizational reengineering, budget management, marketing, and all facets of quality, process, and quality improvement. Excellent background in employee development, training, and leadership. Outstanding analytical, planning, organization, and negotiation skills.

Desire a position in leadership and management that will provide a challenging opportunity to significantly contribute to a company's efficiency, organization, growth, and profitability.

EDUCATION
Graduate Diploma in Banking
GRADUATE SCHOOL OF BANKING
UNIVERSITY OF NEW YORK, New York, New York

Associate of Science in Banking
STATE TECHNICAL INSTITUTE, New York, New York

Basic, Standard, General & Advanced Certificates
AMERICAN INSTITUTE OF BANKING

National Commercial Lending School
UNIVERSITY OF COLORADO, Boulder, Colorado

Diploma in Banking
NEW YORK BANKERS SCHOOL
STERN UNIVERSITY, New York, New York

Bachelor of Science in Business Administration
COLORADO STATE UNIVERSITY, Fort Collins, CO

ADVANCED TRAINING & DEVELOPMENT
Radar Training, American First Bank
RPM Training, American First Bank
Leadership NOW, American First Bank
Teambuilding, American First Bank
LEAP & Appraisals, American First Bank
Diversity, American First Bank

■ **FIGURE 3.7 CONTINUED**
Evelyn Blythe's Scannable Resume with Key Words Highlighted (Page 2)

EXECUTIVE BANKING EXPERIENCE

Senior Vice President
CREDIT REVIEW DIVISION - AMERICAN FIRST BANK, New York, New York - 1973 to Present
Company Track Record of Success: Began with bank in 1973 as a Commercial Loan Officer, and
consistently advanced to positions of higher levels of responsibility and authority due to
outstanding job performance and strong commitment Branchincluded
Regional Commercial Loan Manager (1980 to 1987), Branch Manager for Special Assets Bank
(1987 to 1992), CRO & Private Client Specialist (1992 to 1995), State Manager of Tennessee Credit
Review (1995 to 1996), and current position as Senior Vice President.

Senior Vice President: Hold full responsibility for the operations of the banking institution.
Responsible for examining and analyzing commercial lending units and commercial portfolios. In
charge of reviewing and approving the underwriting documents to ensure they conform to
corporate lending policies. Analyze and advise on credit originating in commercial lending units.

Public Speaking: Facilitate numerous meetings and seminars and speak publicly concerning
banking practices, rules, regulations, and methods.

Committees & Special Projects: Appointed to several high-profile committees including Diversity
Planning Council Member, Business Advisor for INROADS corporate interns, AUV Task Force,
Policies & Procedures Task Force, and Associate Incentive Plan Administration.

Company Reengineering: Selected as a member of the Reengineering Project Team for the
Private Client Group. As part of senior management group, responsible for restructuring and
reengineering management practices for this Private Client Group, which streamlined operations
and increased efficiency.

Manager of New York Credit Review: Managed and directed overall credit review. Assisted in
developing and writing the bank's comprehensive lending and credit policies and procedures for
American First Bank.

Personnel & Supervision: Interviewed, hired, trained, and supervised Credit Review Officers,
Relationship Managers, Special Asset Officers, and Administrative Assistants. Delegated work
responsibilities and monitored overall job performances to ensure accuracy and adherence to
specifications, standards, rules, and regulations.

Budget Management: Review, analyze, and administer budget for operating expenditures.
Review monthly and year-end financial reports and analyze budget variances. Initiate appropriate
strategies to more aggressively control expenditures and changes in organizational structures.

Branch Manager for Special Assets Bank: Held full responsibility for managing overall branch
operations and for collections of problem and delinquent accounts.

Portfolio Management: Reviewed and monitored loan portfolios, serving as Examiner in Charge
(EIC) or Credit Review Officer (CRO) for various exams in and out of State of New York. Held full
responsibility and decision-making authority for establishing and ensuring corporate policy. Led a
team of officers and managed portfolio consisting of manufacturing, agricultural, professional,
executive, wholesale, and retail loans.

■ **FIGURE 3.8**
Evelyn Blythe's Cover Letter with Key Words Highlighted

EVELYN Q. BLYTHE
1111 Anywhere Street
City, State 10000
www.internetprovider.com/~blythe
Phone Number

Are you looking for a highly motivated, goal-oriented Executive to become a leader in your organization? I am confident that, with my experience, training, and commitment to success, I can significantly contribute to your company's team of professionals. For your review, I have enclosed a personal resume that provides details concerning my background and credentials.

As you will note in my resume, I am not a beginner but rather a seasoned professional with more than 24 years of experience building and leading integrated operations within a large national banking institution. My areas of expertise and qualifications include the following:

Proven track record of success in all facets of management, negotiations, corporate policy development, and finanacial analysis.

In-depth experience in examining and analyzing commercial lending units and commercial portfolios. Led a team of officers and managed portfolio consisting of manufacturing, agricultural, professional, executive, wholesale, and retail loans.

Have served as Examiner in Charge (EIC) and Credit Review Officer (CRO) for various exams in and out of state of New York.

Successfully managed and administered multimillion-dollar budgets and initiated appropriate strategies to aggressively control expenditures.

Proactive leader with effective team-building skills. Empower associates to think and work independently and in a team environment, which increases employee morale, productivity, and efficiency.

Proven ability to define issues, propose solutions, and implement changes.

I sincerely believe that, with my experience and career aspirations, I would be an asset to your organization. I would appreciate an opportunity to meet with you to discuss your upcoming plans and long-term goals, along with how my leadership and management abilities could be instrumental in achieving success for your company.

Thank you in advance for your time and consideration. I look forward to speaking with you soon.

Sincerely,

Evelyn Q. Blythe

Make sure you can complete the following e-mail–related tasks before you begin job searching. These exercises will help you use e-mail to network!

- Send an e-mail message to a new recipient.

- Send an e-mail message to someone already on your recipient list.

- Add a name and an e-mail address to your recipient list.

- Receive and view e-mail messages sent to you (In box).

- View all messages you have already sent or scheduled to send (Out box).

- Delete e-mail from your In box or Out box.

- Attach a file (like your resume) to an e-mail message.

- Send one e-mail message to several people on your recipient list simultaneously.

- Send a copy of an e-mail to another recipient in addition to your main addressee (cc or carbon copy).

■ **TABLE 3.3**
Exercises for Learning to Use E-mail

something gets lost or skewed in the transfer. This is a particularly important consideration with resumes, since so many different kinds of word processing programs exist and just as many versions are available within each program. The newer versions read the older versions, but the older versions don't always read the newer ones—and the smaller programs don't convert at all, while the larger programs might . . . and on and on. You get the picture.

The risk is too great that the Heart & Soul resume you so carefully designed will just be a garbled mess of coding and nonsense for the receiver. The answer to this problem is to put your resume in a text file.

Text File Resumes Are Universal

HEART & SOUL TIP

Internet users understand that text file resumes and even scanned resumes don't support appealing design work or formatting, so don't worry about sending a "bland"-looking resume. What is important is that your resume is written and prepared from your heart and soul, because that shows through no matter how the formatting looks.

You can send your resume and cover letter in a file that is so universal that any computer using any program will be able to read it exactly as you sent it. Text files don't contain any formatting or impressive design work, but they can effectively get your message across on e-mail—unimpaired! You can copy your text file resume version into your e-mail message without attaching a document. This will help ensure that the receiver sees all of your resume without having to open and view it through a word processing program.

Seasoned computer users know that you can save a copy of an existing document as a text file. Simply open your resume document, click the "Save As" command, and choose "Text Only" from the drop-down list "Save As Type." Each word processor program might have subtly different commands, but the basic steps to save your document as a text file should be similar.

When you close and reopen your new text version of your resume, you will notice some distinct differences in the layout. Your tabs, alignments, font styles, font sizes, and other formatting will be gone. To make your resume a little more presentable, you might consider realigning some words and sentences so they are better situated on the page. Make sure, however, that you don't insert any formatting commands other than spaces or line breaks. If you insert any commands that a text file doesn't understand, you will have to convert your file to a text file again (and lose the formatting you just tried to insert). It can be confusing, so it's best to keep the file as simple as possible. Text files do not recognize the following:

- Word wraparound
- Special fonts and characters
- Tabs
- Any alignment other than left-aligned

Let's look at Evelyn Blythe's resume after we converted it to a text file (see Figures 3.9 on pages 68 and 69, and Figure 3.10 on page 70). Remember, if you are positive that your receiver has the same word processing program as you do, you can send the original file of your resume. Otherwise, send a text file!

Creating Your Own Resume/Web Site

You can attract attention on the Web by developing your own Web site. Direct your target audience to your Web site for more information about yourself. In addition to your address, e-mail address, and phone and fax numbers, you can also add your Web site address to your list of data. This is a wonderful marketing tool. There's no need to worry about limited use of graphics or formatting, as in your scannable text file resume. On your Web page, you can include full-color photos, images, and text.

Don't be misled by thinking that employers will start knocking on your door just because you have your own Web page. More than likely, you won't get very many unsolicited hits unless you aggressively market your Web page or offer unique skills that keep you in very high demand. Generally, your Web page will be used as a tool to supplement your scanned file, text file, and physical resumes. Often you may pique an employer's interest with a cover letter and resume, but instead of calling, the employer might visit your Web site for more information. So your Web page becomes another opportunity for you to market and sell yourself.

■ **FIGURE 3.9**
Evelyn Blythe's Text File Resume (Page 1)

EVELYN Q. BLYTHE
1111 Anywhere Street
City, State 10000
www.internetprovider.com/~blythe
Phone Number

EXECUTIVE PROFILE

High-caliber, successful Banking Executive with more than 24 years of experience building and leading integrated operations within a large national banking institution, serving both commercial and retail business markets. Promoted rapidly through a series of increasingly responsible positions to final assignment as Senior Vice President of American First Bank. Introduced innovative lending, real estate financing, commercial banking, and operating policies/procedures that positively impacted revenue, profit, and portfolio growth. Appointed to several high-profile committees including Diversity Planning Council Member.

Strong general management qualifications in business analysis and operations, financial market analysis, organizational reengineering, budget management, marketing, and all facets of quality, process, and quality improvement. Excellent background in employee development, training, and leadership. Outstanding analytical, planning, organization, and negotiation skills.

Desire a position in leadership and management that will provide a challenging opportunity to significantly contribute to a company's efficiency, organization, growth, and profitability.

EDUCATION   Graduate Diploma in Banking
    GRADUATE SCHOOL OF BANKING
    UNIVERSITY OF NEW YORK, New York, New York

    Associate of Science in Banking
    STATE TECHNICAL INSTITUTE, New York, New York

    Basic, Standard, General & Advanced Certificates
    AMERICAN INSTITUTE OF BANKING

    Diploma in Banking
    NEW YORK BANKERS SCHOOL
    STERN UNIVERSITY, New York, New York

    Bachelor of Science in Business Administration
    COLORADO STATE UNIVERSITY, Fort Collins, CO

ADVANCED TRAINING & DEVELOPMENT
    Radar Training, American First Bank
    RPM Training, American First Bank
    Leadership NOW, American First Bank
    Teambuilding, American First Bank
    LEAP & Appraisals, American First Bank
    Diversity, American First Bank

■ **FIGURE 3.9 CONTINUED**
Evelyn Blythe's Text File Resume (Page 2)

Senior Vice President
CREDIT REVIEW DIVISION - AMERICAN FIRST BANK, New York, New York, 1973 to Present

• Company Track Record of Success: Began with bank in 1973 as a Commercial Loan Officer, and consistently advanced to positions of higher levels of responsibility and authority due to outstanding job performance and strong commitment to success. Positions have included Regional Commercial Loan Manager (1980 to 1987), Branch Manager for Special Assets Bank (1987 to 1992), CRO & Private Client Specialist (1992 to 1995), State Manager of Tennessee Credit Review (1995 to 1996), and current position as Senior Vice President.

• Senior Vice President: Hold full responsibility for the operations of the banking institution. Responsible for examining and analyzing commercial lending units and commercial portfolios. In charge of reviewing and approving the underwriting documents to ensure they conform to corporate lending policies. Analyze and advise on credit originating in commercial lending units.

• Public Speaking: Facilitate numerous meetings and seminars and speak publicly concerning banking practices, rules, regulations, and methods.

• Committees & Special Projects: Appointed to several high-profile committees including Diversity Planning Council Member, Business Advisor for INROADS corporate interns, AUV Task Force, Policies & Procedures Task Force, and Associate Incentive Plan Administration.

• Company Reengineering: Selected as a member of the Reengineering Project Team for the Private Client Group. As part of senior management group, responsible for restructuring and reengineering management practices for this Private Client Group, which streamlined operations and increased efficiency.

• Manager of New York Credit Review: Managed and directed overall credit review. Assisted in developing and writing the bank's comprehensive lending and credit policies and procedures for American First Bank.

• Personnel & Supervision: Interviewed, hired, trained, and supervised Credit Review Officers, Relationship Managers, Special Asset Officers, and Administrative Assistants. Delegated work responsibilities and monitored overall job performances to ensure accuracy and adherence to specifications, standards, rules, and regulations.

• Budget Management: Review, analyze, and administer budget for operating expenditures. Review monthly and year-end financial reports and analyze budget variances. Initiate appropriate strategies to more aggressively control expenditures and changes in organizational structures.

• Branch Manager for Special Assets Bank: Held full responsibility for managing overall branch operations and for collections of problem and delinquent accounts.

• Portfolio Management: Reviewed and monitored loan portfolios, serving as Examiner In Charge (EIC) or Credit Review Officer (CRO) for various exams in and out of State of New York. Held full responsibility and decision-making authority for establishing and ensuring corporate policy. Led a team of officers and managed portfolio consisting of manufacturing, agricultural, professional, executive, wholesale, and retail loans.

References Available Upon Request

■ **FIGURE 3.10**
Evelyn Blythe's Text File Cover Letter

EVELYN Q. BLYTHE
1111 Anywhere Street
City, State 10000
www.internetprovider.com/~blythe
Phone Number

Are you looking for a highly motivated, goal-oriented Executive to become a leader in your organization? I am confident that, with my experience, training, and commitment to success, I can significantly contribute to your company's team of professionals. For your review, I have enclosed a personal resume that provides details concerning my background and credentials.

As you will note in my resume, I am not a beginner but rather a seasoned professional with more than 24 years of experience building and leading integrated operations within a large national banking institution. My areas of expertise and qualifications include the following:

• Proven track record of success in all facets of management, negotiations, corporate policy development, and financial analysis.
• In-depth experience in examining and analyzing commercial lending units and commercial portfolios. Led a team of officers and managed portfolio consisting of manufacturing, agricultural, professional, executive, wholesale, and retail loans.
• Have served as Examiner in Charge (EIC) and Credit Review Officer (CRO) for various exams in and out of state of New York.
• Successfully managed and administered multimillion-dollar budgets and initiated appropriate strategies to aggressively control expenditures.
• Proactive leader with effective team-building skills. Empower associates to think and work independently and in a team environment, which increases employee morale, productivity, and efficiency.
• Proven ability to define issues, propose solutions, and implement changes.

I sincerely believe that, with my experience and career aspirations, I would be an asset to your organization. I would appreciate an opportunity to meet with you to discuss your upcoming plans and long-term goals, along with how my leadership and management abilities could be instrumental in achieving success for your company.

Thank you in advance for your time and consideration. I look forward to speaking with you soon.

Sincerely,

Evelyn Q. Blythe

HEART & SOUL TIP

Make sure that your Internet account with your ISP allows you to have a Web site. Most of them do!

HEART & SOUL TIP

Use your Web page as a savvy marketing tool. Remember, as soon as you upload your Web page to your ISP, anybody in the world with Internet access can visit your site and learn all about you!

Designing your own Web page is not difficult. Many new software programs can help you create your own site, so you don't have to know any programming codes at all. The most difficult part is not in the design, but in uploading your new creation to your ISP so everybody else on the Web can visit your site. After you fully develop your page, call your ISP customer service line for help. The process is not complicated, but for first-timers it can be a little confusing. After you've done it once with help, you can execute it by yourself as often as you need to.

Marketing your personal Web site is as simple as including your Web site address on your resume, cover letter, and personal business cards. As you submit your resume to companies and on-line job databases, you might have additional opportunities to include your Web site address. Notice that all of Evelyn Blythe's resumes and letters also include her Web site address.

Outline Your Web Site Before You Design It

```
                    ┌─────────────────────────────┐
                    │         Home Page           │
                    │  Executive Summary, Address, │
                    │  Phone Numbers, and E-mail   │
                    └─────────────────────────────┘
```

| Chronological Work History and Educational Background | Career Highlights and Accomplishments | Photo and Personal Bio | References and Letters of Recommendation |

HEART & SOUL TIP

If you have a portfolio, you can publish the entire piece on your Web site. Just make sure your Web page is well organized, so if visitors don't want to learn about your every little accomplishment, they don't have to.

Before creating your personal Web site, you should create a "flow chart." In this example, the home page acts as the doorway to each major subheading. This visual organization of your on-line promotion will help you tremendously as you get into the details of your Web site design. Keep each page simple. If you have too much clutter on any one page, break it up into as many subheadings as you need to. We recommend keeping it as simple as possible, especially if you have never designed a Web page before.

Consider the Size of a Computer Screen in Your Design

Remember, you can't read an entire 8.5 x 11-inch sheet on your average computer screen. In fact, at 100% view, you can see only about 4 to 6 inches of a page, depending on the screen and the resolution. So in your design, you might try to limit the length of each page. The best-designed Web pages allow the reader to see all the important points on one screen. Make sure your Web page/resume allows the reader to see the main points of each page on one screen.

Figure 3.11 illustrates Evelyn's personal Web page. You can copy this format for your own page or use it to generate ideas to create your Web page. Our general recommendation, as with your resume, is to keep your Web site conservative, simple, and professional. Avoid gimmicks and cute tricks unless you are absolutely positive they are appropriate. Lengthy Web sites are fine as long as they are well organized for the visitor.

Using Multimedia Resumes—The Next Wave

A multimedia resume is definitely impressive because it incorporates text, images, and video and audio clips, and it works with or without the Internet. While costly to prepare, multimedia resumes do get attention and can be extremely effective in marketing yourself in the right circumstances. Developing a resume like this is far beyond the scope of this book for several reasons, however. First, it requires programming and/or advanced computing skills, which are not relevant or even necessary for a successful Heart & Soul Internet job search. Second, a multimedia resume/presentation would be overkill for a majority of companies. (For example, what video clips would an accountant want to incorporate into her multimedia presentation? We can't think of any.)

HEART & SOUL TIP

Unless your work or profession is creative and/or in the public eye (advertising, media entertainment, etc.), you don't need to send a multimedia resume or publish video or sound clips on your Web page.

If you're in a creative field, such as advertising or entertainment, a multimedia presentation is perfectly appropriate. It's easy to develop one with a slide presentation software program (usually included in "Office" or "Suite" software packages). You can send the slide show on disk, and the receiver won't need to have the same program you wrote it on to see your presentation. If you include video or sound, you will probably have to send a removable disk or CD. The small 3.5-inch disks don't have enough storage space for most presentations.

If you want to include video and sound in your resume, the easiest and least expensive way to accomplish this is to include it on your Web site. Again, you'll need some advanced knowledge or a good Web page design program to help you accomplish this. Your Web site visitor will also have to have certain equipment and software on his or her computer to be able to view and listen to the audio and video as you had intended.

■ **FIGURE 3.11**
Evelyn Blythe's Web Page

Evelyn Q. Blythe

BANKING EXECUTIVE

| Chronological Work History and Educational Background | Career Highlights and Accomplishments | Photo and Personal Bio | References and Letters of Recommendation |

E-MAIL EVELYN Q. BLYTHE

EVELYN Q. BLYTHE
1111 Anywhere Street
City, State 10000
www.internetprovider.com/~blythe
Phone Number

EXECUTIVE PROFILE

HEART & SOUL TIP

Notice how all of the main points of this Web page can be seen within a height of 4 inches. This top section will fit perfectly on the reader's computer screen.

High-caliber, successful Banking Executive with more than 24 years of experience building and leading integrated operations within a large national banking institution, servicing both commercial and retail business markets. Promoted rapidly through a series of increasingly responsible positions to final assignment as Senior Vice President of American First Bank. Introduced innovative lending, real estate financing, commercial banking, and operating policies/procedures that positively impacted revenue, profit, and portfolio growth. Appointed to several high-profile committees including Diversity Planning Council Member.

Strong general management qualifications in business analysis and operations, financial market analysis, organizational reengineering, budget management, marketing, and all facets of quality, process, and quality improvement. Excellent background in employee development, training, and leadership. Outstanding analytical, planning, organization, and negotiation skills.

Desire a position in leadership and management that will provide a challenging opportunity to significantly contribute to a company's efficiency, organization, growth, and profitability.

Work History & Education
Evelyn Q. Blythe
Return to Home Page
Career Highlights and Accomplishments
Photo & Personal Bio
References & Letters of Recommendation
E-mail Evelyn Q. Blythe

■ **FIGURE 3.11 CONTINUED**
Evelyn Blythe's Web Page

Work History & Education

EVELYN Q. BLYTHE

| Return to Home Page | Career Highlights and Accomplishments | Photo and Personal Bio | References and Letters of Recommendation |

E-MAIL EVELYN Q. BLYTHE

EDUCATION

Graduate Diploma in Banking
GRADUATE SCHOOL OF BANKING
UNIVERSITY OF NEW YORK, New York, New York

Associate of Science in Banking
STATE TECHNICAL INSTITUTE, New York, New York

Basic, Standard, General & Advanced Certificates
AMERICAN INSTITUTE OF BANKING

Diploma in Banking
NEW YORK BANKERS SCHOOL
STERN UNIVERSITY, New York, New York

Bachelor of Science in Business Administration
COLORADO STATE UNIVERSITY, Fort Collins, CO

ADVANCED TRAINING & DEVELOPMENT

Radar Training, American First Bank
RPM Training, American First Bank
Leadership NOW, American First Bank
Teambuilding, American First Bank
LEAP & Appraisals, American First Bank
Diversity, American First Bank

Senior Vice President
CREDIT REVIEW DIVISION - AMERICAN FIRST BANK, New York, New York, 1973 to Present

Company Track Record of Success: Began with bank in 1973 as a Commercial Loan Officer, and consistently advanced to positions of greater responsibility: Regional Commercial Loan Manager (1980 to 1987), Branch Manager for Special Assets Bank (1987 to 1992), CRO & Private Client Specialist (1992 to 1995), State Manager of Tennessee Credit Review (1995 to 1996), and current position as Senior Vice President.

■ **FIGURE 3.11 CONTINUED**
Evelyn Blythe's Web Page

Highlights/Accomplishments

EVELYN Q. BLYTHE

| Chronological Work History and Educational Background | Return to Home Page | Photo and Personal Bio | References and Letters of Recommendation |

E-MAIL EVELYN Q. BLYTHE

Senior Vice President: Hold full responsibility for bank operations. Responsible for examining and analyzing commercial lending units and commercial portfolios. In charge of reviewing the underwriting documents to ensure they conform to corporate lending policies. Analyze and advise on credit originating in commercial lending units.

Public Speaking: Facilitate numerous meetings and seminars and speak publicly concerning banking practices, rules, regulations, and methods.

Committees & Special Projects: Appointed to several high-profile committees including Diversity Planning Council Member, Business Advisor for INROADS corporate interns, AUV Task Force, Policies & Procedures Task Force, and Associate Incentive Plan Administration.

Company Reengineering: Selected as a member of the Reengineering Project Team for the Private Client Group, which streamlined operations and increased efficiency.

Manager of New York Credit Review: Managed and directed overall credit review. Assisted in developing and writing the bank's comprehensive lending and credit policies and procedures for American First Bank.

Personnel & Supervision: Interviewed, hired, trained, and supervised Credit Review Officers, Relationship Managers, Special Asset Officers, and Administrative Assistants.

Budget Management: Review, analyze, and administer budget for operating expenditures. Review monthly and year-end financial reports and analyze budget variances. Initiate appropriate strategies to more aggressively control expenditures and changes in organizational structures.

Branch Manager for Special Assets Bank: Held full responsibility for managing overall branch operations and for collections of problem and delinquent accounts.

Portfolio Management: Reviewed and monitored loan portfolios, servicing as Examiner In Charge (EIC) or Credit Review Officer (CRO) for various exams in and out of State of New York. Held full responsibility and decision-making authority for establishing and ensuring corporate policy. Led a team of officers and managed portfolio consisting of manufacturing, agricultural, professional, executive, wholesale, and retail loans.

■ **FIGURE 3.11 CONTINUED**
Evelyn Blythe's Web Page

Personal Bio

EVELYN Q. BLYTHE

| Chronological Work History and Educational Background | Career Highlights and Accomplishments | Return to Home Page | References and Letters of Recommendation |

E-MAIL EVELYN Q. BLYTHE

- Willing to travel up to three days per week.
- Willing to relocate anywhere in the United States.
- Also fluent in French, German. Traveled extensively throughout Europe.
- Play cello in popular local string quartet.
- Enjoy team activities and sports.
- Ranked in top 50 tennis players (in my age bracket) in my city.
- Love outdoors, reading about American history, and spending time with my family.

■ **FIGURE 3.11 CONTINUED**
Evelyn Blythe's Web Page

Letters of Recommendation

EVELYN Q. BLYTHE

| Chronological Work History and Educational Background | Career Highlights and Accomplishments | Photo and Personal Bio | Return to Home Page |

E-MAIL EVELYN Q. BLYTHE

I have worked with Evelyn for over 10 years and, without a doubt, she is the most dynamic and results-oriented executive I have ever had the fortune to work with. I highly recommend her to anyone lucky enough to get her on their team!

BILL BERNSTEIN, CFO, AMERICAN FIRST BANK

BILL'S PHONE NUMBER

When it comes to understanding every facet of the commercial banking business, Evelyn is the most qualified executive I know. I have been in the banking business for over 25 years and honestly can't think of anyone more impressive and more knowledgeable in this industry!

SALLY MAYFIELD, VICE PRESIDENT, AMERICAN FIRST BANK

SALLY'S PHONE NUMBER

Evelyn is an intelligent, warm, and generous person. I will always admire her work and her giving attitude toward her work and any activity or event she is involved in.

JESSE HOLCOLMB, PREVIOUS BRACH MANAGER, AMERICAN FIRST BANK

JESSE'S PHONE NUMBER

Use this chart to help you schedule time to develop the following resumes you will use in your Heart & Soul Internet job search. Remember, once you write your first resume, the other versions are easy!

Type of Resume	Use/Application	Time to Develop
Physical Resume	Mailing, networking	2 to 6 hours
Scannable Resume	Mailing to companies that scan resumes	15 minutes
Text File Resume	E-mail resume to companies, contacts, on-line job databases discussion groups, etc.	15 minutes
Personal Web Site	Allow employers to learn more about you	1 to 4 hours*
Multimedia Resume	Send to companies for maximum impact & attention	Varies

*Web site development can take more time for the inexperienced.

■ **TABLE 3.4**
Resume Development Time Chart

No matter what your profession or trade is, we recommend that you prepare a Heart & Soul resume, scannable resume, text file (electronic) resume, and your own Web site (see Table 3.4). So prepare all your resumes, organize your different electronic versions, and get ready for our next secret!

Finding Your Ideal Employer on the Internet

Once you make a decision, the universe conspires to make it happen.

RALPH WALDO EMERSON

AFTER YOU HAVE PREPARED your Heart & Soul resume job search tools, you're ready to research and compile a target list of your ideal employers, which is Secret #4 for a successful Heart & Soul Internet job search. It's crucial to being proactive in your Heart & Soul campaign. You don't want to wait for a job to fall into your lap; instead, you want to actively pursue the kind of job you'll love! That's the only way to obtain a higher-caliber career position that will make you happy and career fulfilled.

This proactive job search is based on your ability to identify and locate the employers you want to target in your job campaign. You don't have to wait for a decent advertisement to show up in the newspaper or even on-line. Be assertive and be proactive! You can research and find the companies you want to work for before they start soliciting candidates for that dream job you've been looking for!

If you don't yet know exactly what the ideal job would be, maybe you need a little more time or a little more help. Don't take the first offer that comes along. We've seen too many people take jobs based on short-term needs, without defining what they really want to do. The consequences are often the same—they're unsatisfied and unhappy. By doing your research before you look for a job and by defining the specific kind of company you want to target, you can find the job that's right for you! You can have the kind of life you want and the kind of life you dream about. In fact, that's the only kind of life worth living. If you don't know what your life and career dreams are, we urge you to practice creative visualization, do your homework, and uncover your heart's desires.

HEART & SOUL TIP

Don't confuse multiple job offers with career success. If job offers are coming often and easily, you most likely are making yourself accessible to a class of jobs beneath your skill level. You should go for more! Reach for the stars! Reach for your heart's dream!

In today's competitive marketplace, you can't simply settle for finding only one ideal employer. You need to identify 25, 50, 200, or even 2,000 potential ideal employers. A successful job search can often be an odds game. You might have to target and contact many employers just to get a few interviews and maybe one good solid job offer. The more employers you target, the better your chances of finding your dream job!

At first, you might have trouble identifying appropriate employers to target. Don't worry about this. In the initial phases of your employer research, you don't have to decide whether you want to work for a certain company; you're simply deciding whether you want to *explore* working for that company and find out more about it. Since this is a numbers game, try to talk to (or approach) as many different companies as possible. You'll never know what sorts of opportunities exist until you ask!

HEART & SOUL TIP

Job searching is just like marketing: you may have to approach 25, 50, or even 1,000 companies before you get the one offer you're looking for!

Later we'll discuss how to approach and contact these employers; for now we'll look at how to find them in the first place. You want to work for a company that will fulfill your dreams and heart's desires, right? But how do you know if a particular company will do that? The right company not only provides the kind of work you'll love, but it also employs the kind of people you'll enjoy working with. The right company will respect you and empower you to achieve your best. You have unique skills, attributes, and needs, and you could work in many different kinds of environments. Unfortunately, you can't research Internet databases to find companies that will accommodate all your emotional needs. You have to be realistic and utilize a more practical method of researching potential employers. As you surf the Web and career Web sites, make a note of interesting employers that are out there recruiting for employees. Visit their Web sites and consider adding them to your list of potentials.

Internet Employer Databases

Begin your research by basing your search for the ideal employer on tangible criteria that are readily available, inexpensive, and easily accessible. All major Internet employer databases (which can also be found on CD-ROM or in a reference book) categorize their listings by industry, location, and size (both by sales and by number of employees). By narrowing down your criteria using these simple categories, you can eliminate hundreds or even thousands of nonideal companies from your job search. In a city of 75,000 employers, for example, you could effectively narrow down your target list to a few hundred, based only on these basic and simple criteria. From this manageable list of employers, you can begin the task of in-depth researching that will help you further eliminate nonideal employers.

After you determine the criteria for your target employer, you'll use an employer database that will best serve your needs. You can easily locate and download employer information on-line. Several major employer databases and their Web site addresses are included in Appendix II of this book.

These companies are in the business of selling information, and some information is free. These databases will provide the employer's address, phone number, and key contacts. Some databases are costly, but they'll provide you with contacts' addresses and hard-to-find company data, while others are inexpensive, yet they provide only the company name and address. Other options for gaining employer information include purchasing association membership lists, business direct mailing lists, telephone books, client lists of certain companies, chamber of commerce lists, your alma mater's alumni directory, and industry directories. Of course, each of these database organizations will have a Web site that you will want to visit for more information.

HEART & SOUL TIP

When targeting employers on the Web, first identify and define basic criteria for your "ideal" employer by industry, location, and size (number of employees and sales volume).

Supplement lists generated from a database with your own personal thoughts about the companies you want to target (if they are not already included on your list). As you research and further develop your target list, you will eventually compile an "A" list of employers, any of whom you'd be proud to work for!

We know that researching companies by "industry classification" sounds quite mechanical and doesn't sound like a Heart & Soul function, but how else can you create an objective list of companies to target? Even mechanical and technical functions can incorporate Heart & Soul. You've got to seek out good employers on your own, whether they are hiring or not!

Using Two-Digit SIC Codes for Type of Industry

Most Internet employer databases are defined by SIC (Standard Industry Classification) codes as defined by the U.S. Department of Commerce. Each specific industry is categorized by a four-digit code, where the first digit represents the broad industry division, the second represents a subset of the first, the third is a subset of the second, and so on. We recommend that you start with the two-digit SIC codes we have included in this book. If you need more detail, go to your local library and ask for the complete list of SIC codes. These go into more detail than you should ever need.

In Table 4.1, check each two-digit code representing the type of industry you would like to consider in your job search. If you have several tiers of interests, consider marking each category as an "A," "B," or "C" priority. You will use this list not only to generate job searching ideas, but also as a reference when you search for employers in databases.

Considering Geographic Location

Location is another important factor to consider. Where do you want to work? Where would you be willing to work, given a good offer? You need to know these things before you start researching employers.

In Worksheet 4.1 on page 84, mark the state(s) in which you want to target employers. If you have more specific criteria, most databases will search using ZIP codes, counties, cities, and metro areas (metro areas are defined as the city and all the surrounding counties) as well. Again, if you have several tiers of priorities, mark them "A," "B," and "C."

If you have no geographic preferences, just leave this blank. In your searches, you can include all of the states or international destinations as possible criteria for your potential employers.

Considering Size of Business
(by Number of Employees and/or Sales Volume)

You can also define your target employer by its size. Do you want to work for a small company or a large company? Given your particular profession and industry of choice, where are the majority of opportunities? For most employees, the small and midsized companies offer the most potential. Usually the key decision maker is more accessible in a small or midsized company than in a large, national organization. But you should select the size for which you are best suited.

At the most basic level, the size of your potential employer can be inferred by the number of its employees and/or the amount of its annual sales. Use

Agriculture, Forestry, Fishing (01–09)
Agricultural Production Crops (01)
Agricultural Production - Livestock (02)
Agricultural Services (07)
Forestry (08)
Fishing, Hunting, Trapping (09)

Mining (10–14)
Metal Mining (10)

Construction (15–17)
General Building Contractors (15)
Heavy Construction, except Building (16)
Special Trade Construction (17)

Manufacturing (20–39)
Food and Drink Products (20)
Textile Mill Products (22)
Apparel and Other Textile Products (23)
Lumber and Wood Products (24)
Furniture and Fixtures (25)
Paper and Allied Products (26)
Printing and Publishing (27)
Chemicals and Allied Products (28)
Petroleum and Coal Products (29)
Rubber and Misc. Plastic Products (30)
Leather and Leather Products (31)
Stone, Clay, and Glass Products (32)
Primary Metal Industries (33)
Fabricated Metals Products (34)
Industrial Machinery & Equipment (35)
Electronic and Other Equipment (36)
Transportation Equipment (37)
Instruments and Related Products (38)
Misc. Manufacturing (39)

Transportation, Communication, Utilities (40–49)
Railroad Transportation (40)
Local Passenger Transit (41)
Trucking and Warehousing (42)
United States Postal Service (43)
Water Transportation (44)
Transportation by Air (45)
Pipelines, except Natural Gas (46)
Transportation Services (47)
Communication (48)
Electric, Gas, and Sanitary Services (49)

Wholesale Trade (50–51)
Wholesale Trade Durable Goods (50)
Wholesale Trade Nondurable Goods (51)

Retail Trade (52–59)
Building Materials/Garden Supplies (52)
General Merchandise Stores (53)
Food Stores (54)
Automotive Dealers and Service Stations (55)
Apparel and Accessory Stores (56)
Furniture and Home Furnishing (57)
Eating and Drinking Places (58)
Misc. Retail (59)

Finance, Insurance, and Real Estate (60–67)
Depository Institutions (60)
Nondepository Institutions (61)
Security and Commodity Brokers (62)
Insurance Carriers (63)
Insurance Agents, Brokers, and Services (64)
Real Estate (65)
Holding and Other Investment Offices (67)

Services (70–89)
Hotels and Other Lodging Places (70)
Personal Services (72)
Business Services (73)
Auto Repair, Services, and Parking (75)
Misc. Repair Services (76)
Motion Pictures (78)
Amusement and Recreation Services (79)
Health Services (80)
Legal Services (81)
Educational Services (82)
Social Services (83)
Museums, Botanicals, Zoological Gardens (84)
Membership Organizations (86)
Engineering and Management Services (87)
Private Households (88)
Misc. Services (89)

Public Administration (91–99)
Executive, Legislative, and General (91)
Justice, Public Order, and Safety (92)
Finance Taxation and Monetary Policy (93)
Administration of Human Resources (94)
Environmental, Quality, and Housing (95)
Administration of General Economic Programs (96)
National Security and International Affairs (97)
Nonclassifiable Establishments (99)

■ **TABLE 4.1**
Standard Industry Codes

List *states* you would consider in your job search	List by *city, county, 3- or 5-digit ZIP codes*, or specific areas of this state (if applicable)	A, B, or C priority?

■ **WORKSHEET 4.1**
Targeting Employers by Geographic Location

Worksheet 4.2 to identify a range of size criteria to consider. As you do your searches, you may try different variations of these criteria to more accurately produce the number of employers you want to target.

When we help a client prepare a job search campaign, we first target a manageable amount of companies—as few as 50 or as many as 1,500, or more often, 200 to 500 potential employers. We recommend targeting thousands if you can, because the more you target, the better your chances of tapping into a hidden job market and finding the companies that are hiring—or soon will be!

When we search databases, we establish the location and industry preferences first and then try variations of size to get us closer to our goal number. If a client wants to target 500 companies and our initial search of "employers with more than 250 employees and $50 million in sales" retrieves 1,500 employers, we limit our size criteria even more. By doing this, we can eventually retrieve a quantity of target employers that is closest to our goal number.

HEART & SOUL TIP

Searching for potential employers in a database is a "work in progress," and you may have to adjust your search several times to find the companies that are perfect for you!

Number of Employees	✓	Annual Sales	✓
20,000+		$200,000,000+	
15,000 to 20,000		$150,000,000 to $200,000,000	
10,000 to 15,000		$100,000,000 to $150,000,000	
5,000 to 10,000		$75,000,000 to $100,000,000	
2,500 to 5,000		$50,000,000 to $75,000,000	
1,000 to 2,500		$25,000,000 to $50,000,000	
500 to 1,000		$10,000,000 to $25,000,000	
250 to 500		$5,000,000 to $10,000,000	
100 to 250		$2,500,000 to $5,000,000	
50 to 100		$1,000,000 to $2,500,000	
25 to 50		$500,000 to $1,000,000	
10 to 25		$250,000 to $500,000	
Less than 10		Less than $250,000	

■ **WORKSHEET 4.2**
Targeting Employers by Size of Business

Using Worksheet 4.2, check the categories you would like to consider. Use the number of employees and annual sales to indicate the size of your prospective employer.

Check the categories you would like to consider in your job search. Use this worksheet as a "work in progress." You may want to adjust your criteria as your employer research progresses.

Cole Barrington

Cole was a sharp young industrial engineer who had done some consulting with some major accounting firms. He had done the same kind of work for the last seven years and was really getting anxious to move on to something else. With his exposure to many companies and operating styles, he felt as though he could be a real asset to the right organization.

Cole had been working primarily with companies in the northeastern United States, but his wife's family lived in southern California and he had promised her that they would relocate so they could raise their newborn son, Josh, near her family. His problem, he told us, was that he didn't know of any appropriate companies in southern California. He was confident in his ability to get interviews and job offers once he knew what companies to approach.

We helped him with several areas of his job search, but finding the contacts and companies was the most important area in which he needed help. We told Cole that to do a good search for potential employers, we would need to get a better idea of what his ideal employer should be.

We showed him the list of SIC codes and asked him to pick the industries he wanted to target. He hadn't even looked at the list for two seconds when he said, "That's it! Number 35, Manufacturing—Industrial Machines and Equipment." Usually this process takes a little more time, but Cole knew exactly what he wanted in his next job. So we quickly moved on to other criteria to select his ideal employer.

After we confirmed that his geographic preference was the southern California area, we asked him about the size of the company. We told him he could gauge size by the number of employees, annual sales, or both. He wasn't really sure about the best company size, but he imagined any firm with more than 250 employees would be worth considering.

"Great," we told him. "Give us a few minutes and let's see what we can dig up." But we searched our databases and found only 32 potential companies in his desired area. Since we always recommend targeting as many employers as possible, we suggested alternatives to finding additional employers to target.

Because he was sure of the industry he wanted to pursue, we asked him if he would consider smaller companies and maybe a broader geographical area than just southern California. Cole said that there was no way he could talk his wife out of living in that area, so the only option we had was to target smaller companies (which he said he wouldn't mind anyway).

If Cole had been doing the research himself, we would have instructed him to explore the Web sites of the employer databases we have noted in Appendix III. We also would have had him research the Web sites of the local chamber of commerce trade association for membership lists. Because so many of our clients are busy with hectic lives, we research companies for them. For Cole's particular situation, we accessed a database from Dun & Bradstreet. Although many fine employer databases are available, this one worked best for Cole's needs and budget.

After we reduced the minimum number of employees to 100, we found more than 150 companies to target. Although this is still a relatively small number, with Cole's highly specialized skills we thought 150 might just be the perfect number for him to target in his job search campaign.

After we mailed one of Cole's resumes to the CEO or president of each company, he began to visit each employer's Web site. Cole told us that our online research helped him tremendously. When he was researching each company's Web site, he said he found other important contacts as well as helpful information regarding company trends, opportunities, and hiring practices. Within six weeks he had set up 12 interviews and had received his first acceptable job offer. He was very excited and pleased (to say the least).

Deborah Macintosh

Deborah Macintosh came to us discouraged and not very full of hope. She wanted to find a position as an executive director with a reputable organization or nonprofit, preferably in New York, but she just didn't know where to start. Figures 4.1 (page 88) and 4.2 (pages 89–90) show Deborah's "before" resume that she provided us and the "after" resume we rewrote for her, and Figure 4.3 (page 91) shows the cover letter we wrote to accompany her revised resume.

Deborah was thrilled with her new resume but was still concerned about how to find the companies to target. We assured her that her resume was only one piece of the Internet job search puzzle, and now she needed to make some decisions about how to narrow down her search to a manageable subset of target employers—*before* she went on-line! Tables 4.2 through 4.4 (pages 92–93) list the criteria we developed together.

Deborah wanted to do her own Internet employer research but wanted us to show her how. We gave her all the tips and advice she needed to get started. We contacted her later to see how she had done in her Internet job search. She said that after she had the focus and the job search tools, she did well. It took her a while to check out all the different employer databases, but finally she located a few good ones. Through the Internet, she told us, she found a company that specialized in business lists in the area she wanted. She said lots of companies sold business lists, but she really had to do her research to find a company that she trusted. After she put together her target list of employers, she visited each organization's Web site. She submitted her resume on-line whenever possible and then followed up by sending a physical copy in the mail. If she couldn't submit her resume on-line, she said she still found plenty of addresses and helpful contacts and would mail her paper resume accordingly. After two more months of aggressive job searching, she had four acceptable offers.

HEART & SOUL TIP

You should always research the companies before interviewing with them. After all, just as the companies want to make sure you're right for them, you want to make sure they're right for you.

As with our candidates in this chapter, it's important that you research employers on the Internet. You should always research the companies before you interview with them. After all, you want to make sure they're right for you, just as the companies want to make sure you're right for them!

Employers are increasingly searching the Internet for employees as a way to find talent in a shrinking labor pool. They see it as a cost-effective way to broaden their search, in addition to buying traditional classified ads in newspapers.

■ **FIGURE 4.1**
Deborah Macintosh's "Before" Resume

Deborah Macintosh
1411 Anywhere Street
City, State 10000
Phone Number

Education **Bachelor of Arts in Sociology - Minor: Criminology, COLUMBIA**

UNIVERSITY, New York, New York

Work History

Executive Director, TRAVEL COMPANION, New York, New York - 1996 to Present
Develop state-of-the-art reservations. Designed a Web Site to promote company and its services.
In charge of marketing. Develop and execute comprehensive Direct Mail Marketing plans to increase
business. Interview, hire, train and supervise Field Managers. In charge of budget.

Regional Director, AIR EXPRESS, INC., Newark, New Jersey - 1994 to 1996
Developed business plans. Achieved 100% reliability in operations, airport services, airport performance
safety, customer service, and baggage handling.
Opened 12 new markets. Responsible for managing account calls, presentations and contract negotiations.
Initiated a Pay for Performance Incentive Program. Received the Company & Associates Team Award.

Operational Manager, CORPORATE EXPRESS, INC., Denver, Colorado - 1993 to 1994
Responsible for employee performance evaluations, passenger service, ground operations, safety, and
customer service training. Planned a program to cross-train employees. Utilized 40% of labor work force.
Originated a Structural Orientation Program for new hires to orient them into company's standards, polices
and procedures.

Corporate Lead Rover, CARRIER EXPRESS, INC., Las Cruces, New Mexico - 1992 to 1993
Responsible for working in a variety of areas including passenger & ground services, customer service and
operations. Analyzed and restructured OJT (on-the-job training). Implemented the Rover Program.

DEBORAH MACINTOSH
1411 Anywhere Street
City, State 10000
Phone Number

Professional Objective & Profile

Goal-oriented, multitalented Executive Director is seeking a position with a national organization or nonprofit that will fully utilize more than seven years of experience building and leading integrated operations for major companies. Have held highly visible leadership positions and have earned a reputation for continually making a positive bottom-line difference by reengineering operational practices. Consistently successful in restructuring overall operations to minimize and maintain costs and increase profitability. Talented in developing and leading business opportunities and marketing strategies to maximize growth and profitability. A proactive leader with excellent team-building and training skills. A strong motivator with experience as a public speaker at conferences and in the schools. Strong general management qualifications in business operations, financial analysis, and all facets of process/productivity/quality improvement.

EDUCATION
Bachelor of Arts in Sociology—Minor: Criminology
Columbia University, New York, New York

Professional Experience

Executive Director
TRAVEL COMPANION, New York, New York, 1996 to Present

■ *Company Analysis & Management:* After taking over as Executive Director, investigated and analyzed company's financial performance record. Launched a companywide reengineering and market repositioning to meet company expectations for revenue growth and profit improvement. Reengineered management practices to streamline operations and increase productivity 40 percent.

■ *Systems & Program Development:* Spearheaded the development and launching of a progressive state-of-the-art reservations service that increased efficiency and productivity. Designed and created a Web site to promote the company and its services.

■ *Marketing & Advertising:* Through creating and developing innovative marketing and organizational strategies, successfully positioned Travel Companion as one of the leading companies in the U.S. among the largest airline carriers in the world. Develop and execute comprehensive Direct Mail Marketing plans to increase business.

■ *Business Development:* Responsible for managing new business development and strategic planning to maximize growth and profitability. Established growth plans for individual accounts and personally managed account calls, presentations, and contract negotiations.

■ *Personnel & Supervision:* Interview, hire, train, and supervise Field Managers.

■ *Budget Management:* Manage, analyze, and project $4.4 million budget for operating expenditures within the company. Analyze budget variances and initiate appropriate guidelines to more aggressively control expenditures.

■ **FIGURE 4.2**
Deborah Macintosh's "After" Resume (Page 2)

Professional Experience

Regional Director
AIR EXPRESS, INC., Newark, New Jersey, 1994 to 1996

- *Management:* Managed and directed overall operations and administration for the region.

- *Company Analysis & Development:* Researched and analyzed company's declining areas as well as profitability ratios. Developed business plans to improve new city openings, expansion sites, and overall operations. Restructured company's management practices and achieved 100 percent reliability in operations, airport services, airport performance safety, customer service, and baggage handling.

- *Company Growth:* As a result of formulating policies and procedures to develop innovative marketing and business plans for company expansion, successfully opened 12 new markets. Responsible for managing account calls, presentations, and contract negotiations.

- *Program Development:* Created and initiated a Pay for Performance Incentive Program that increased employee morale, productivity, and efficiency.

- *Awards:* Received the Company & Associates Team Award for outstanding team performance.

Operational Manager
CORPORATE EXPRESS, INC., Denver, Colorado, 1993 to 1994

- *Management:* Managed overall operations and administration for this company. Conducted ongoing analyses to evaluate the company's efficiency and cost-effectiveness. Responsible for employee performance evaluations, passenger service, ground operations, safety, and customer service training.

- *Company Reengineering:* After reengineering company's management practices, was successful in incorporating 123 operational flights and increasing staff to 160 employees to accommodate company's growth.

- *Training:* Developed and implemented a program to cross-train employees, which minimized and maintained labor costs, and successfully utilized 40 percent of labor work force to increase productivity.

- *Program Development:* Originated a Structural Orientation Program for new hires to orient them into company's standards, policies, and procedures.

Corporate Lead Rover
CARRIER EXPRESS, INC., Las Cruces, New Mexico, 1992 to 1993

- *Troubleshooter:* Responsible for troubleshooting the western division of United Express, Mesa Airlines, USAir Express, America West Express, and all subsidiary operations of Mesa, Inc. Researched and identified problems and implemented creative problem-solving techniques to resolve issues. Responsible for working in a variety of areas including passenger and ground services, customer service, and operations.

- *Training:* Restructured training procedures to more effectively accommodate corporate merger. Analyzed and restructured OJT (on-the-job training), which improved the company's training program.

- *Program Development:* Developed and implemented the Rover Program, which increased employee efficiency and productivity.

Deborah Macintosh's Cover Letter

DEBORAH MACINTOSH
1411 Anywhere Street
City, State 10000
Phone Number

> *Place the specific name
> and address here.*

It is my understanding that you are looking for a highly motivated, goal-oriented Executive Administrator. I am confident that, with my background in executive administration, public speaking, and leadership positions, I can significantly contribute to your team of professionals. For your review, I have enclosed a personal resume that will provide you with details concerning my background and credentials.

As you will note, I am not a beginner, but rather a seasoned professional with more than seven years of experience building and leading integrated operations for major companies. My areas of expertise and qualifications include the following:

- Proven track record of success in management, business development, program development, and personnel management.

- Talented in restructuring and reengineering operations and programs that yield reduced company costs and increased profitability.

- Proactive leader with effective team-building skills. Empower associates to think and work independently and in a team environment, which increases employee efficiency, productivity, and morale.

- Strong public relations skills with excellent background in public speaking and community affairs.

- Proven ability to define issues, propose solutions, and implement cost-effective as well as profitable changes.

- Financial and analytical expertise in budget development, forecasting, and management.

- Demonstrated leadership, communication, and negotiating skills.

- Proficient in computer systems and applications.

I sincerely believe that, with my experience and career aspirations, I would be an asset to your organization. I would like to request a personal interview at your earliest convenience so we can discuss how I can best contribute to your company's goals.

Thank you in advance for your time and consideration. I look forward to speaking with you soon.

Sincerely,

Deborah Macintosh

Agriculture, Forestry, Fishing (01–09)
Agricultural Production Crops (01)
Agricultural Production - Livestock (02)
Agricultural Services (07)
Forestry (08)
Fishing, Hunting, Trapping (09)

Mining (10–14)
Metal Mining (10)

Construction (15–17)
General Building Contractors (15)
Heavy Construction, except Building (16)
Special Trade Construction (17)

Manufacturing (20–39)
Food and Drink Products (20)
Textile Mill Products (22)
Apparel and Other Textile Products (23)
Lumber and Wood Products (24)
Furniture and Fixtures (25)
Paper and Allied Products (26)
Printing and Publishing (27)
Chemicals and Allied Products (28)
Petroleum and Coal Products (29)
Rubber and Misc. Plastic Products (30)
Leather and Leather Products (31)
Stone, Clay, and Glass Products (32)
Primary Metal Industries (33)
Fabricated Metals Products (34)
Industrial Machinery & Equipment (35)
Electronic and Other Equipment (36)
Transportation Equipment (37)
Instruments and Related Products (38)
Misc. Manufacturing (39)

Transportation, Communication, Utilities (40–49)
Railroad Transportation (40)
Local Passenger Transit (41)
Trucking and Warehousing (42)
United States Postal Service (43)
Water Transportation (44)
Transportation by Air (45)
Pipelines, except Natural Gas (46)
Transportation Services (47)
Communication (48)
Electric, Gas, and Sanitary Services (49)

Wholesale Trade (50–51)
Wholesale Trade Durable Goods (50)
Wholesale Trade Nondurable Goods (51)

Retail Trade (52–59)
Building Materials/Garden Supplies (52)
General Merchandise Stores (53)
Food Stores (54)
Automotive Dealers and Service Stations (55)
Apparel and Accessory Stores (56)
Furniture and Home Furnishing (57)
Eating and Drinking Places (58)
Misc. Retail (59)

Finance, Insurance, and Real Estate (60–67)
Depository Institutions (60)
Nondepository Institutions (61)
Security and Commodity Brokers (62)
Insurance Carriers (63)
Insurance Agents, Brokers, and Services (64)
Real Estate (65)
Holding and Other Investment Offices (67)

Services (70–89)
Hotels and Other Lodging Places (70)
Personal Services (72)
Business Services (73)
Auto Repair, Services, and Parking (75)
Misc. Repair Services (76)
Motion Pictures (78)
Amusement and Recreation Services (79)
Health Services (80)
Legal Services (81)
Educational Services (82)
Social Services (83)
Museums, Botanicals, Zoological Gardens (84)
Membership Organizations (86)
Engineering and Management Services (87)
Private Households (88)
Misc. Services (89)

Public Administration (91–99)
Executive, Legislative, and General (91)
Justice, Public Order, and Safety (92)
Finance Taxation and Monetary Policy (93)
Administration of Human Resources (94)
Environmental, Quality, and Housing (95)
Administration of General Economic Programs (96)
National Security and International Affairs (97)
Nonclassifiable Establishments (99)

■ **TABLE 4.2**
Deborah Macintosh's Standard Industry Codes List

List *states* you would consider in your job search	List by *city, county, 3- or 5-digit ZIP codes,* or specific areas of this state (if applicable)	A, B, or C priority?
New York	Manhattan	A
Southern California	Anything south of San Francisco	B
Texas	Houston	C

■ **TABLE 4.3**
Deborah Macintosh's Geographic Criteria

Number of Employees	✓	Annual Sales	✓
20,000+	✓	$200,000,000+	✓
15,000 to 20,000	✓	$150,000,000 to $200,000,000	✓
10,000 to 15,000	✓	$100,000,000 to $150,000,000	✓
5,000 to 10,000	✓	$75,000,000 to $100,000,000	✓
2,500 to 5,000	✓	$50,000,000 to $75,000,000	✓
1,000 to 2,500	✓	$25,000,000 to $50,000,000	✓
500 to 1,000	✓	$10,000,000 to $25,000,000	✓
250 to 500	✓	$5,000,000 to $10,000,000	✓
100 to 250	✓	$2,500,000 to $5,000,000	✓
50 to 100	✓	$1,000,000 to $2,500,000	
25 to 50	✓	$500,000 to $1,000,000	
10 to 25		$250,000 to $500,000	
Less than 10		Less than $250,000	

■ **TABLE 4.4**
Deborah Macintosh's Size of Business Criteria

In Table 4.2, for Deborah we selected only SIC code 86. We determined that the organizations and nonprofits she defined would primarily be in this category. We knew that although some target employers might not fall into this category, this would be an excellent start. In Table 4.4, many membership organizations and nonprofits are not about sales, so that category, while helpful, is not as relevant as is the number of employees. Deborah told us that any organization with more than 25 employees would be great. So to be safe, we chose all organizations employing more than 25 people.

More and more, newspapers are responding to the Internet by posting their classified ads on-line. Dozens of free sites on the Net allow headhunters, employment agencies, and job seekers alike to find one another easily and efficiently in a way that was impossible just a few years ago. Some of these sites even link employers with colleges, which is the next-best thing to on-site recruiting.

The Internet has brought the world's employers to home PCs. Individuals can now look for jobs virtually anywhere in the world, any time of day, increasing the choices of an already mobile, transient workforce. With each new day, more advances are on the way for Internet job seekers.

New software is currently being developed that will let job seekers type in their desired position, salary, location, and other requirements and have their PCs hunt the Web for suitable jobs. The software will alert users when the search is done and keep the list on file. Someday, as we become a more entrenched technological society, everyone will search for jobs on the Internet!

HEART & SOUL TIP

More and more, newspapers are responding to the Internet by posting their classifieds on-line.

5 Making a Heart & Soul Connection

Destiny is not a matter of chance, it is a matter of choice; it is not a thing to be waited for, it is a thing to be achieved.

WILLIAM JENNINGS BRYAN

NETWORKING AND INTERVIEWING are the greatest Internet skills you can master. This is where your efforts in career planning, resume writing, and employer research pay off. This is where you finally want to be—in front of someone who can influence your goals. It is our fifth secret for conducting a successful Heart & Soul Internet job search.

Networking on the Internet

Networking is a great tool in any kind of job search, but with the widespread use of the Internet, it is much easier now than it ever was before. Effective networking benefits you in the following ways:

- Helps you add to your list of target "ideal" employers
- Gives you insight into departments, companies, and industry trends and changes
- Provides you with access to key decision makers who can either refer you or hire you
- Allows you to stay motivated and interested in a proactive and ongoing effort to reach your goals

Networking works! We all feel a greater comfort level around our friends and our friends' friends. We are more open to conversation after a common introduction. For example, through a friend, you may meet someone who works in a company you're targeting. You ask your new acquaintance if he or she could hand-deliver your resume to a few important people, or at least pass on a good word. Because of the personal introduction, your resume takes on a new importance within the company. You establish credibility (if even in the slightest way) that others sending their resumes cold wouldn't be able to do. You have immediately been categorized as a higher-tier potential candidate—not that the job is yours, but your odds of getting it have improved dramatically.

During your networking activities, you should search for *information* as well as job leads. Each person you speak to on the Internet (or in person) will be able to help you in a particular way. Sometimes you may not want to mention anything more than, "If you hear of some opportunities in . . . let me know." Generally speaking, however, you want to dig as deep as possible to find out as much information as you can. That means you want to circulate, mingle, and investigate every source imaginable. In addition to your on-line networking, you should also network off-line, by going to chamber of commerce meetings, working out at popular fitness centers, joining special interest groups, or volunteering to work free for community organizations. The more you are "out and about," the more opportunity you'll have to meet people and nurture relationships that will be beneficial to you!

In addition to informally networking through friends, clubs, and meetings, you should set up appointments with "key players" and influential people as often as possible. These appointments can come in the form of a lunch or even a quick e-mail message—whatever is applicable to each person. Just make the connection!

Many of these networking meetings are considered *informational interviews,* which are much easier to get than actual job interviews. If you e-mail or call someone to discuss trends and opportunities within an industry, and *not* to solicit a job offer, the e-mail or meeting takes on a more informational and friendly tone.

To begin your networking efforts, make a list of everyone you know and their e-mail addresses. Prioritize them according to who you think could help

HEART & SOUL TIP

In the business world, networking is a natural part of life. It's O.K. to "use" all the contacts you can to help you find a good job. Just remember, the next time someone comes to you for networking, help him or her out any way you can—giving back to others is the true Heart & Soul way!

you most in your job search. Don't make too many assumptions about who will help you and who won't. You'll be surprised at what information you'll pick up from your most casual acquaintances. Make some personal business cards. Instead of a company or title, you might consider adding your area or specialty, such as "Marketing Manager," "Writer," "Programmer," or whatever best describes the job you're seeking.

In this instance, it's definitely O.K. to "use" your friends and associates to help you find jobs or make important contacts. Later, when someone comes to *you* asking for help, return the favor. The more you give to life, the more life will give back to you. This is a simple law of life. Don't forget this when you're enjoying that wonderful new career and are successful and happy. Plus, don't forget this simple law of life even when you're down and struggling. After all, giving to others when you're happy and successful is *easy*. It's your ability to help others when you're struggling that really counts.

Next, make a list of key decision makers or influential people you don't know but who would be good contacts. Your target list of employers that you researched in Chapter 4 will make excellent contacts. This list of employers should include the key contact (usually the president, owner, or CEO) of each company, the company's Web site address, and the e-mail addresses of important contacts. Also, think of any popular, political, or influential people you could call. You never know who might be able and willing to help.

Each day you should make a number of new calls based on your proactive plan of action (which you'll create in Chapter 6). As you contact each person on your list, ask her or him to refer three colleagues who might be of some assistance. Then add these three new names to your list of contacts. Your list could get very long, but as you progress in your job search, you'll begin to hone in on key contacts and opportunities that seem most promising.

Make sure you balance your networking with an equal amount of "warm" and "cold" contacts each day. Warm contacts represent all the people you know or with whom you share in common a friend or acquaintance. Cold contacts could be the decision makers in your target employer list or influential people in your chosen profession or industry. If you're uncomfortable networking with people you don't know, your job search may be hindered. Stretch yourself! Take a chance and call those people who have never heard of you. Introduce yourself, and ask them for some advice. What have you got to lose? Nothing, except perhaps a great job or job lead!

Now that we have discussed the benefits of networking, let's explore how to network on-line. First, make a list of warm contacts in Worksheet 5.1 (page 98). Then make a list of cold contacts in Worksheet 5.2 (page 99).

HEART & SOUL TIP

Before you establish a face-to-face or Internet "networking" meeting with someone, ask yourself how this person could help you most. What information and experience does this person have that could be beneficial to you?

HEART & SOUL TIP

Your networking calls and contacts can be divided into two main categories:
■ Warm Contacts. Friends, family, colleagues, decision makers you know personally, or direct referrals from any of these people.
■ Cold Contacts. Decision makers, influential people, or anyone else that you don't already know who may even remotely be able to help you.

HEART & SOUL TIP

Stretch yourself! Call contacts who have never heard of you! Make new friends!

LIST OF WARM CONTACTS

HEART & SOUL TIP

Don't forget to ask each contact for a few other contacts who might be able to help!

Name	Phone	E-mail		Name	Phone
1.				21.	
2.				22.	
3.				23.	
4.				24.	
5.				25.	
6.				26.	
7.				27.	
8.				28.	
9.				29.	
10.				30.	
11.				31.	
12.				32.	
13.				33.	
14.				34.	
15.				35.	
16.				36.	
17.				37.	
18.				38.	
19.				39.	
20.				40.	

■ **WORKSHEET 5.1**
List Your Warm Contacts

LIST OF COLD CONTACTS

HEART & SOUL TIP

What other people could help you that are not on your targeted research list?

Name	Phone	E-mail		Name	Phone
1.				21.	
2.				22.	
3.				23.	
4.				24.	
5.				25.	
6.				26.	
7.				27.	
8.				28.	
9.				29.	
10.				30.	
11.				31.	
12.				32.	
13.				33.	
14.				34.	
15.				35.	
16.				36.	
17.				37.	
18.				38.	
19.				39.	
20.				40.	

■ **WORKSHEET 5.2**
List Your Cold Contacts

Internet Networking Works!

The single greatest asset of the Internet is that millions of people exchange information and ideas on-line each day. Many people are out there (some not even on your networking list) who could potentially help you in some way. Experts, colleagues, decision makers, people with similar concerns, and friends are all available with a single click of your mouse. It's a great way to network and is probably one of the most underrated job-searching resources available.

If you're like many people in our fast-paced world, you may complain that you don't have time to do traditional networking. Or maybe you don't feel comfortable calling people on the telephone and discussing employment opportunities. On the Net, you can "meet" more people in an hour than you could meet off-line in a year.

Of course, as with any communication effort, you must apply strong communication strategies to ensure that you make good contacts and get free, first-hand job market or business information. Your success with on-line communication depends on your ability to effectively communicate what you need while being sensitive to your contact's time and other resources. Each time you use your modem, you must know *exactly* what you want to accomplish and assertively communicate this to your audience.

HEART & SOUL TIP

Write your messages and postings in clear, appropriate, and professional business English. You may feel like you're alone in front of your computer, but you're not. You will be making tens, hundreds, or even thousands of first impressions each time you communicate on-line. Remember, first impressions count!

Once on-line, contact can be made through e-mail, e-mail mailing lists, discussion groups, newsgroups, or chat lines, many of which will be focused around your industry, career field, or subject. Too many on-line networkers convert their sometimes slightly sloppy off-line communication skills to the Internet. This isn't good, because they have just exposed their bad communication skills to a new, larger *worldwide* audience, and that could be embarrassing. On the Internet, your audience is unlimited.

Your on-line networking goal is to reach the most qualified people possible and motivate them to assist you. Just as a persuasive phone call can entice decision makers to help you, strong communication skills can help on the Internet. When venturing out into cyberspace to post messages and to network with people in your industry, remember and follow these rules:

- Don't ask questions that have no point or meaning. Be direct and clear in your questions.
- Write in a friendly, warm, and interesting tone.
- Make sure you direct your chat or e-mail message to the right person or post your article (or question) to the right newsgroup.
- Be organized and thorough about the goals of your search.
- Always follow up on any communication on the Internet. Utilize proper "netiquette" and don't neglect to say thank-you.
- Be appreciative and communicate a tone of gratitude in all communication.

For instance, you wouldn't want to post a message like this one on-line:

Subject: Sales/Marketing Position
From: DANN
Experienced sales rep seeks position in LA, California.

Ho-hum! Hey, somebody keep us awake! This person probably won't get many responses to the message that he posted on a message board. He obviously put no thought or effort into the message. Where's his heart and soul? Doesn't he realize that people will be reading this message? Would you be interested in talking to him? Not likely. A better way to write this message would be:

Subject: Pharmaceutical Sales/Marketing Position in Los Angeles, CA
From: DANN
Hello Friends in Los Angeles!

A results- and profit-oriented Sales Representative, with more than 15 years of experience marketing and selling pharmaceuticals, is seeking a position in the Los Angeles area. Consistently ranked in the top 5 in the company on national basis. Any help or contacts would be greatly appreciated. Would be willing to help provide you with contacts in southeastern United States. E-mail me soon and let's talk!

Thank you in advance for your time,

David Nivens

This second message communicates interest, friendliness, appreciation, and success. It's more reflective of his heart and soul. If you make people feel as though their opinions matter, you will be surprised at how most people will help. If you don't reflect the Heart & Soul approach in your message, many people who could be a resource to you simply won't feel needed and will move on to someone else on-line. When you're using a Heart & Soul approach, you must always remember that people are your most important resource and must be treated with respect and good manners. Don't approach people on the Internet as though they're machines.

It's not easy to solicit help from anyone, and that's true on the Internet, as in life. You want to motivate your contact on the Internet, as you would on the telephone, to help you. So don't forget these simple commonsense facts when you're making contacts through on-line networking.

See Table 5.1 (page 102) for some helpful exercises for learning to network on-line.

If you're new to the Internet, practice the following before you network on-line.

Before you begin aggressively job searching on-line, these tips can help you become comfortable with on-line travel!

- Explore 20 Web sites of major national companies. Make notes about what you like and dislike about each company.

- Search for sites involving your favorite hobby. Travel to at least 20 sites and print the most interesting information you can find about a particular subject.

- E-mail 10 friends (back and forth) at least five times each. Also, attach a file of your resume (upload) or other similar document to your e-mail message.

- Join five e-mail mailing lists.

- Visit 10 USENET newsgroups and post at least 10 articles (comments or messages) on any subject that interests you.

- Drop in on a chat line at least 10 times.

■ **TABLE 5.1**
Exercises for Learning to Network On-line

E-Mail	Regular Mail
Quick, easy, and inexpensive. (Winner)	Slower, cumbersome, and inexpensive.
Easily deleted.	Must be physically thrown away. (Winner)
Very easy to respond to. (Winner)	Difficult to respond to.
Offers voice and video features. (Winner)	Will pretty much always just be mail.
Best for shorter documents.	Can send formal, legal, and large documents. (Winner)
Overall Winner: E-mail!	

■ **TABLE 5.2**
E-mail versus Regular Mail

Use Electronic Mail (E-mail) to Help You Network

E-mail is a fast, convenient, and affordable way to communicate with anyone who also has an e-mail address, anywhere in the world. This tool will be a fundamental part of your Heart & Soul Internet job search. No more playing phone tag! Just send your e-mail, wait a day, and see what you get back.

Be careful, however. If you send an unsolicited e-mail message, you run the risk of not getting a return message. Try to make a personal connection with whomever you are contacting by mentioning a mutual friend or colleague. This will help ensure that your e-mail gets read and gets a response. See Table 5.2 for a comparison of e-mail versus regular mail.

Effective E-mail Networking

Several forms of Internet networking are available besides e-mail (discussion groups, e-mail mailing lists, chat lines), but our recommendation is to learn to use e-mail first. This medium offers so much to your Internet job search that you can't afford to miss out.

E-mail seems to be the perfect form of communication for networking. When people check their e-mail, they are in the mood to communicate and answer messages. They have made time in their day to quietly read and respond to their e-mail. So no matter when your message was sent, it will be read and potentially answered by the receiver at the appropriate time. What this means is that you won't get "blown off" because your contact is too busy to talk to you on the phone.

One problem in e-mailing a contact, however, is locating an e-mail address in the first place. It seems kind of odd to call for an e-mail address instead of just directly telephoning the contact, doesn't it? Some companies post e-mail addresses on their Web sites, so you should definitely check out their Web sites first. But you may have to call to get a company's Web site address too! So be prepared to do appropriate research for each contact.

Obviously, if the contact is a friend or is easily approachable, you can network with the contact the first time you call and simply follow up with e-mail.

But if your contact is someone you don't know well who works for a large company, you might want to start with a very polite, tactfully written e-mail. You must make a connection with your contact in some fashion for your e-mail to be well received. If possible, mention a mutual acquaintance (perhaps you have a colleague within the industry), refer to a conversation you had with, or a message you received from, someone in the company, or find some other common ground.

HEART & SOUL TIP

E-mail us at:
dpeerce@mindspring.com *or at:*
heartsoul@mindspring.com
and see why it's easy and fun!

Use your first e-mail message as a means to schedule future correspondence. Cold e-mail messages should be brief and to the point. Always ask for a follow-up meeting. Never bombard your contact with a bunch of loaded questions without first introducing yourself. Remember, these e-mail messages are easy to delete. Entice your reader to want to respond to you. Following are a few examples of cold e-mail messages from some of our clients that worked well for them. Tailor what they wrote to suit your personal networking situation.

> **To:** Wendy Crane
> **From:** Susan Smith
>
> **Subject:** Friend of Frank Koch
>
> Ms. Smith,
>
> I believe we have a mutual acquaintance in Frank Koch. He is a vendor for my current employer, JJ Holdings LLC, and he was very complimentary of your knowledge and skills with the "book publishing on demand" technology.
>
> I would love to have the opportunity to ask you a few questions. This is an area that I have researched in depth, and I see so much potential. May I e-mail you a little more about myself and ask a few questions? Or, if you prefer, I can call you at a time that is convenient for you.
>
> Thank you so much!
>
> —Susan

This message is great! It's polite and brief, and it immediately mentions the connection in the Subject line. And in the first sentence, Susan is careful not to ask for "too much."

> **To:** Bob Sullivan
> **From:** Grady Wilson
>
> **Subject:** Fellow Member of IAL Association
>
> Hi Bob,
>
> I am not sure if you remember me, but we met briefly in Houston at the international IAL meeting. I have a few ideas concerning this business we're in. It feels like my business is turning into a commodity operation as opposed to the premium technology venture it was several years ago.
>
> Is there a good time when I can call you, or would you prefer e-mail? It won't take too long, but I think I might be on to something.
>
> Respectfully,
>
> —Grady

Notice that the tone of the message is relative to the relationship—they are both members of a professional association. Because the message is brief and doesn't ask for too much, it successfully entices the reader to want to learn more.

Scott Sheahan

In this scenario, Scott Sheahan wanted to get an interview with Marla Robinson, who was vice president of sales and marketing for Giant Industries. Scott had no contacts at Giant Industries, but he did learn that Marla Robinson was the vice president and the executive decision maker. He had to cold e-mail Marla and try to set up an interview, without sounding like he was soliciting a job.

First Networking E-mail

To: Marla Robinson
From: Scott Sheahan

Subject: Just Read Your Great Article!

Ms. Robinson,

I just read about a recent study that Giant Industries conducted concerning the number of companies that are now rightsizing instead of downsizing. I've been in marketing and sales with the nation's number one company, Commercial Industries, for more than 10 years. But I've recently become interested in your company.

Giant Industries offered some valuable information regarding the projects they're working on to empower and motivate employees. I wonder if I could meet with you sometime to discuss these projects?

Thanks,

—Scott

Second (Returned) Networking E-mail

To: Scott Sheahan
From: Marla Robinson

Subject: RE: Just Read Your Great Article!

Dear Scott,

Thank you, but it's been very busy. I will have to pass for now.

Third Networking E-mail

To: Marla Robinson
From: Scott Sheahan

Subject: Great Article!

Hello Ms. Robinson,

One of the main projects I have worked on for the last five years is on empowering employees to increase productivity in a downsized workplace. My work has been well received by many colleagues, and I would love to speak with you, if only for a few minutes.

I know you are busy, but may I call your secretary, Beth, and set up a 10-minute appointment?

—Scott

Fourth (Returned) Networking E-mail

To: Scott Sheahan
From: Marla Robinson

Subject: RE: Great Article!

Dear Scott,

O.K., but wait until next week to come in. I'll be out of town this week.

The Networking Meeting

If you can convince someone you've just e-mailed to meet with you, you've made significant progress in networking. Once Scott was able to establish a meeting with Marla Robinson, the executive decision maker, he had to make sure he was ready for this meeting. First, he made sure that he had all his job-searching tools ready. He made copies of his resume (so that Ms. Robinson could pass them on to other decision makers) plus several copies of his list of references, a leather-bound notebook for note-taking, and a couple of pens. (You should always have an extra pen handy in case the person you're talking to needs one.) In addition, since he'd done his homework, he took along some reports and notes about what he believed he could do for the company. He knew that any new ideas or projects he'd created could win him "brownie points" at this networking meeting.

Here's how Scott's networking meeting went:

"Hello Ms. Robinson, I'm Scott Sheahan."

"Nice to meet you Mr. Sheahan," Ms. Robinson said as she offered her hand to Scott. "Won't you please sit down? Now, tell me what you'd like to discuss concerning Giant Industries."

"First of all," Scott began, "thank you so much for seeing me today. I appreciate this and I won't take too much of your time. I brought along some reports and graphs that illustrate strategic measures for company rightsizing as opposed to downsizing. I thought you might find them interesting."

From this moment on, Ms. Robinson was hooked. She wanted to hear more about Scott's ideas and, after talking for a while, she assured him that Giant Industries might have a position for him in the "near future."

HEART & SOUL TIP

Being polite, but persistent, with your e-mails can successfully win you interviews!

After this networking meeting, Scott wrote Ms. Robinson a thank-you e-mail and then followed up with e-mail and phone calls whenever it was appropriate. Because he was persistent and kept in touch, he won another interview and was hired within two months at Giant Industries.

Not all stories will end this way. Sometimes a networking meeting is just a chance to talk, and nothing more. But sometimes it's an actual job interview, so be prepared for anything.

Network Even When You Don't Think You Should Be Networking

At times, you might try to forget about your job search to alleviate some of the stress that naturally develops, but we want to caution you never to forget totally or ignore your responsibility to network with someone who might be able to help you. Keep your eyes and ears on alert all the time. You never know—an important decision maker might be shopping in the same aisle as you today at the grocery store. Always have a few business cards handy and a few key questions on the tip of your tongue.

Even if you don't "talk business" with someone when you see her or him out casually or socially, you still have the opportunity to make some sort of personal, albeit brief connection. The next day, you can call that person and use your recent interaction as a reason to call. For example, *"Bob, after I saw you at the park with your kids, I had a few thoughts about our industry. Would you mind if I stopped by on Wednesday for about 10 minutes? I have some ideas I'd like to bounce off of you."* Of course, remember to temper your formality to reflect how well you know the contact.

Network On-line with Internet E-mail Mailing Lists

E-mail mailing lists can be an integral part of your on-line networking. After you join an e-mail mailing list, you will periodically receive messages regarding that group's focus. Unlike with a newsgroup (which we will discuss next), where you must visit the group's site to get messages, all sorts of messages and information will be sent straight to your e-mail address when you join an e-mail mailing list. Most of these lists require that you first get information before subscribing. You can do this by sending a message to the address provided with the word *information* in the body of the message. If problems occur, a help message containing pertinent commands will be directed back to you.

The trick to making the Internet work for you and your career is to find and join the right e-mail mailing list. Unfortunately, due to the rapid pace of change on the Internet, we can't provide the names of the lists you should join, but we can certainly tell you how to find the good lists. For finding e-mail lists, newsgroups, and chat lines, we recommend visiting ***http://www.liszt.com*** or ***http://www.reference.com.*** Look in Appendix II for more specific resources on e-mail mailing lists and Web pages.

Since the Web is evolving by the minute, we also recommend checking out all of the major search directories (also known as search engines), such as **Yahoo, InfoSeek, Lycos, Excite, Alta Vista, Hot Bot, Web Crawler,** and the others listed in Appendix II. These sites will help you find current and relevant information on the Web.

We would like to caution the new Internet user, however. If you are yet to gain significant experience on the Web, you need to set aside several hours on-line to learn about e-mail mailing lists, newsgroups, and chat lines.

For News Groupies, Try a Newsgroup (or USENET)

Newsgroups are also called USENETs (user networks). Even though newsgroups are considered part of the Internet, they are not part of the World Wide Web. To better understand newsgroups, think of a single bulletin board posted in an area that attracts only people with the same interests. For example, a bulletin board posted at a comic book shop will have all sorts of notes about old and new comic books. As you might imagine, these notes will be read only by comic book readers. Newsgroups come under the umbrella of "discussion groups," which also include e-mail mailing lists.

Newsgroups are similar to that bulletin board. Someone in a specific newsgroup will post a message, an idea, a question, or a critique that is called an *article*. As you read the article, you are given an opportunity to reply. Your reply is posted (as on a bulletin board) so others can read the original article as well as your reply. Other readers can then respond to both the original article and your answer.

USENET newsgroup articles are not read in a pictorial/graphical way, as are many Internet resources. They are simple messages written in regular text, just like a printed letter. Beginners tend to avoid this resource because of its no-nonsense and nonflashy method of communication. Don't make that mistake! You can uncover some great opportunities, network with others, and obtain important information in these newsgroups, so plan on incorporating them into your daily Internet job search.

A newsgroup's name consists of two or more words, separated by periods. The first word tells what the general topic of interest is, like "biz" for business. All the words that follow serve as subcategories to the main heading. Newsgroups are referenced by abbreviations, much like a Web site is referenced with a URL. You should be able to tell from the initials alone what topic is featured in the newsgroup. See if you can guess what these newsgroups are about:

Bermuda.jobs.offered
Houston.jobs.offered
Euro.jobs
NYC.jobs.offered

For fun and practice on the Internet, locate your newsreader on your Web browser or a comparable program and explore different newsgroups.

All newsgroups are divided into categories to make them easier to find. Look for these abbreviations for the following categories:

alternative	alt
business	biz
computers	comp
miscellaneous	misc
recreation	rec
social	soc

Most newsgroups keep only current articles posted and regularly purge the system of old or unwanted messages. The most popular Web browsers also have built-in newsreaders that are very easy to use. Check your documentation, search on-line, or call your customer service line for more information about newsreaders.

HEART & SOUL TIP

You can uncover some great opportunities, network with others, and obtain important information in newsgroups, so plan on incorporating them into your daily Internet job search.

When you click on a newsgroup, read the FAQ (frequently asked questions) first. This will give you the answers to commonly asked questions, so when you begin posting and responding to articles, you will avoid making "rookie" comments and errors. Not that it's bad to be a rookie—but remember, you want to reflect intelligence, savvy, and professionalism as you network on-line. Make sure that your article is relevant to the specific newsgroup. Nothing irritates readers more than wading through an unrelated article. (It's a waste of time!) As far as your writing goes, just make sure you use good grammar and "Netiquette" skills, which we'll explain in more detail later on in this book.

In Appendix II, we have included numerous newsgroups that you can visit directly. Other services help you search through newsgroups to find related articles or areas of interest that mirror your needs. Visit any major search engine or **http://www.liszt.com** or **http://www.reference.com** for access to many newsgroups and to search for specific topics. In addition, the main search sites listed in Appendix II could prove valuable in helping you find appropriate newsgroups.

Internet Chitchat

Chatting on the Internet is fun, entertaining, and informative. You may not find a job lead every time you log on, but you can do some fantastic networking and even on-line interviewing. There are several ways to chat on-line. You can visit specially designed Web sites or find the option through your ISP. Simply sign on as instructed, read a few passages as they are typed in by other people, and, when you are ready, type in your own comment.

Before you learn all the ways you can chat on-line, go to your ISP's chat section (if available) or go to a Web site for on-line chatting (such as the "Ichat" site at **http://www.ichat.com** or the site at **http://www.liszt.com**). As you experiment, you will learn that you can video chat and voice chat in addition to typing (or text) chat.

As with newsgroups and e-mail mailing lists, the trick to productively networking using chat lines is to find one that reflects your interests. Again, check out Appendix II for more resources.

About the Formal Interview

The job search process is a lot like running hurdles. The first hurdle: find the employer or job lead. Next hurdle: customize your resume and cover letter for that particular job and company. Next hurdle: the company must select you for an initial interview after you have done your networking. Once you get an interview, the next hurdle appears: you must make a *great* first impression if you want to get asked back for a second interview, and on and on! One hurdle after another. If you don't clear one hurdle, you can't get to the next one, which could lead to the job offer. And the most important hurdle for you to focus on is your next one! Haven't you heard a football coach say, "We're not looking at the championship yet, we're just taking it one game at a time"? That's exactly what you have to do—take it one game, one hurdle, at a time. And an interview is always your last hurdle before you get a job offer.

The Open-Ended Question

Communication issues are a little more complex than appearance issues. The one question that makes or breaks most interviews is usually the first one, "Tell me about yourself." (Don't you just hate it?) You have probably been asked this question before, but still you fidget, sweat, clench your fingers around your briefcase, and feel your heart pound. You're thinking, "Does this employer really want to know about my collection of *X-Files* episodes?" (We doubt it.)

These kinds of questions are broad and open-ended, and they require the interviewee to control the content and the pace of what is being said. Naturally, the employer is trying to determine how you feel about yourself. He or she wants to assess your level of confidence in your work. But this type of question can make even the most confident uneasy at times.

Unrehearsed, your answer can flop. But this is an easy question to answer! The prepared, savvy interviewee will calmly highlight topics that entice the interviewer to want to know more. This, in effect, allows the interviewee (you) to control the interview to some extent. You have the power to introduce topics about yourself that you'd like to discuss. The key word is *preparation*. You simply must practice answering the questions that you might be asked in an interview. There is no shortcut to this! By being prepared, you are able to fully concentrate on the moment at hand. (This is no time to be daydreaming about what you're going to have for dinner that night!)

HEART & SOUL TIP

Be prepared. It's the only way to go to an interview. There is no shortcut to being totally prepared for a job interview!

Your interviewer will watch how gracefully and confidently you handle questions. Did you ramble on and on with no point in sight, or were you too brief, with nothing to say? Did you develop your history well and expand on accomplishments, or did you just chatter nervously about the rain outside or the blue carpet on the floor, or whatever came to mind? An interviewer can learn important clues about your character, confidence level, and philosophy in a very short time, so be prepared!

The open-ended question will come up in different guises again and again. From chatting on-line to your first telephone interview to your final interview with the company president, you will be asked to talk about yourself. You may give the same or a similar answer to several different people. That's O.K.! Each one is meeting you for the first time, so you don't have to think of something new, witty, different, or magical to say to each new person you meet. Write out a good script that introduces your education and work experience and then

HEART & SOUL TIP

Don't be shy about giving the same or a similar answer to an open-ended question to different people. It's O.K. to repeat a great answer.

concentrate on highlighting accomplishments relevant to the job you are seeking. Always be prepared! These are all integral parts of the Heart & Soul Internet job search, so make your lists and practice your answers.

Next, we have included an interview with our client Alexandra Ward that illustrates tough questions and answers that usually come up in interviews. Read her interview and practice being asked these same questions yourself.

"Alexandra, Tell Me About Yourself"

Interviewer, Mr. Randolph: "Good morning Alexandra. Your resume says you just graduated and you have a bachelor's degree in public relations. Why don't you tell me a little bit about yourself."

Alexandra: "That's right, I graduated magna cum laude from the University of Kentucky and I have a Bachelor of Science degree in public relations. I just completed an internship with Randy Gilbert's public relations company in New York, which is ranked as one of the top 10 PR firms in the nation, and found this work to be challenging and exciting. Although my long-term goal is to manage and direct a public relations firm, I am currently looking for an entry-level position that will provide a great avenue to learn all aspects of the business. That's why I'm seeking a position with you at your firm, Mr. Randolph."

Mr. Randolph: "What kind of work do you specifically want to do?"

Alexandra: "I'm a great publicist. I promoted a rock 'n' roll band while I was in college and gained valuable experience working with owners and managers in the entertainment industry. I'm aware that your company handles all the PR for leading entertainment artists and I believe I would be an asset to your staff in an entry-level position in public relations or publicity."

Mr. Randolph: "What are your expectations of us, if we should hire you?"

Alexandra: "I expect to be given the opportunity to learn as much as I can about the industry and to advance to positions of greater responsibility and authority. In the same way, you can expect me to surpass company expectations."

Mr. Randolph: "What work experience has been the most valuable to you and why?"

Alexandra: "As I mentioned, I just completed an internship with one of the largest and most successful PR firms in the nation. This work was valuable

HEART & SOUL TIP

Sell yourself in your interview by mentioning your assets—your special skills and talents.

because it taught me how to work with entertainment artists and all levels of management and personnel. It was a window of opportunity that showed me how exciting public relations and publicity can be."

Mr. Randolph: "What was the most useful criticism you ever received, and who was it from?"

Alexandra: "My college professor told me that I was great with people and very creative when it came to conceptualizing promotional and publicity campaigns. However, he told me that I wasn't very organized and was often too scattered in my approach. This criticism helped me because I then took the necessary steps to become more organized and methodical in my approach to publicity. It greatly helped me when I interned in New York."

Mr. Randolph: "What has been your greatest challenge?"

Alexandra: "Getting the people at the PR firm in New York to accept me and to respect my ideas. Because I was a young college student from Kentucky, they didn't take me very seriously at first. Then, as I continued to offer great ideas for projects and then complete these projects myself, they began to take notice."

HEART & SOUL TIP

Be honest about your weaknesses, but explain how you can turn those weaknesses into strengths. And always, show how you accept challenges to prove yourself even in the most trying situations!

Mr. Randolph: "Describe your leadership style."

Alexandra: "It's really quite simple. I like to empower others to be confident in their own opinions and ideas. This seems to encourage people to achieve their maximum potential. I lead by setting an example—by treating others as I would like to be treated. And I give others the freedom to make mistakes. I don't believe in trying to control their thoughts and actions. It can stifle creativity."

Mr. Randolph: "If I hire you, what can you contribute to this company?"

Alexandra: "My great passion for public relations and my strong commitment to achieving results!"

Mr. Randolph: "We are looking at a lot of candidates; why are you the best person for this job?"

Alexandra: "Because I have no doubt that I'm the best choice."

This interview clearly illustrates a woman who is poised, self-confident, and career-oriented. Because she was prepared, she never faltered for one moment

HEART & SOUL TIP

Always demonstrate self-confidence in your interview.

when asked a question. The public relations company at which she was interviewing handled mostly publicity and PR for entertainment artists. Because she knew this, she highlighted the experience she had gained while working for a similar type of agency in New York. She provided information that directly related to the company's needs.

Later in this chapter we have provided some common on-line and face-to-face interview questions for you to read and answer. Practice, practice, practice!

What About the On-line Interview?

In principle, everything that applies to a face-to-face interview applies to an Internet interview, with a few exceptions. First, if you don't have video or audio capability on your computer, you certainly don't have to worry about your appearance or intonation. Next, if you are interviewing via a live chat line or a private Internet meeting room, you must be careful not to write long sentences. You need to be concise and succinct in your on-line communication. However, if your interview is going back and forth via e-mail, you have more time to write all the information you need, and you shouldn't worry about writing in brief statements.

We are often asked how one sets up an on-line interview, but the answer is really up to the employer. Many companies maintain a chat site on their own Web page that they can use for interviewing, while others may direct you to a certain area on the Web. Our advice is to familiarize yourself with chat lines, e-mail, and general on-line interviewing, and be as flexible as you can about the interview. Some employers prefer telephone over face-to-face interviewing, but be aware that how you are interviewed is not your decision. If the employer instructs you to use a certain chat line or Internet meeting room at a certain time and date, we recommend that you visit there before your interview to familiarize yourself with the Web site.

Let's look at an example on-line interview as it progresses on a chat line.

Betty Vandela

Betty was looking for a desktop publishing position with a major publishing firm. She was clearly focused, had effectively targeted her audience, had networked, and had narrowed down her options to five major publishing firms. She was beginning to get interviews and job offers, when one company she'd found on the Web set up a live Internet interview. She had aggressively utilized the Internet in her job search but hadn't yet done a live interview on-line with someone to whom she had never spoken.

Betty had already been prequalified for the position by Bruce Wilkerson, the hiring decision maker. This on-line interview was her first chance to discuss her qualifications and resume with the company. When she was finished with the interview, she printed the text.

Betty Vandela's On-line Interview with Bruce Wilkerson

Bruce: Betty are you there?

Betty: I'm here Bruce. How are you doing today?

Bruce: Great. I've got just a few questions. So I'll try to be brief. Are you ready to go?

Betty: Sure Bruce. I've been looking forward to this. What can I tell you about myself?

Bruce: Tell me more about your freelance design work. What sort of deadlines were you under?

Betty: Bruce, if there is one thing I know, it's deadlines! Freelancing for two major magazines, I received an assignment often the same day it was due. Rarely did I ever have more than a week to complete the work. I've maintained that workload for more than three years now, so I would have to say that I am excellent with deadlines.

Bruce: Good! I would like to see your portfolio. I only have your resume and a few samples. Can you e-mail me something?

Betty: Absolutely! I can get that to you within an hour after we finish here.

Bruce: I noticed you have done the majority of your work out of your own home. We do that a little bit here, but you would probably have be at our office at least one week a month. Is that a problem?

Betty: No, my husband travels a little now, and we have plenty of domestic help. As long as I have at least a week's notice, I can travel anywhere you need me.

Bruce: Betty, I've checked around a bit, and I know you have a few friends over at one of our competitors. Is that going to be a conflict?

Betty: Bruce, I hold my work in the highest regard, and my friends know that. I know you're probably speaking of Judy Clement. She is a real pro in this business, and while I respect her very much, I wouldn't mind winning a few bids over those of her company. In fact, it might be kind of fun!

Bruce: That's what I like to hear. Can you schedule another meeting with my assistant, Josh? I would like you to meet some key people around the office. This time, I think a full audio/video interview with the whole team might be best. Please call or e-mail Josh tomorrow. He'll set it up with you.

Betty: Sounds great. I'll call him tomorrow, and thanks for the meeting!

Bruce: No problem. I look forward to more. I'm out of here. Have a great day.

Betty: Thanks. Bye!

Get Ready for Tough Questions on the Internet & Face-to-Face

HEART & SOUL TIP

Don't be afraid of tough questions in an interview. Be prepared for them!

We understand that tough questions asked during an interview can drive you crazy and leave you feeling drained. Sometimes it seems as though you've just "confessed" your life history to a complete stranger. An interview can also make you feel quite humble. Not everyone has a gleaming, spotless background. But the way you handle those tough questions and the way you handle yourself can conquer even the toughest interview situation, and you can be a winner at this! So, don't be afraid; just be prepared.

How would you answer the following questions? Try practicing in front of a mirror, or even better, make a video of yourself as you answer these questions. Play back the tape, critique yourself, and practice again!

1. Tell me about yourself.
2. What are your long-term goals?
3. What are your short-term goals?
4. How do you plan to achieve both your short-term and long-term goals?

HEART & SOUL TIP

Have a friend, colleague, or career professional videotape an interview with you, so you can critique your appearance, eye contact, body language, and answers. Make appropriate adjustments and do it again. Practice until you feel totally confident!

HEART & SOUL TIP

You can use an Internet meeting/ chat program like Microsoft NetMeeting to conduct an on-line interview. You can also exchange files and configure the program to reflect your on-line communication needs.

5. Tell me about your hobbies.

6. What are your greatest strengths?

7. What are your greatest weaknesses?

8. If you were independently wealthy and didn't have to work, what would you be doing?

9. What was your favorite job and why?

10. Describe a situation in which you had a conflict with a co-worker and how you handled it.

11. What do you think people like most about you?

12. What do you think people like least about you?

13. How well do you work under pressure?

14. How do you motivate people?

15. Describe your leadership style.

16. What is the most important lesson you have learned in school or out of school?

17. Who do you admire most in your life and why?

18. What accomplishments are you most proud of?

19. What characteristics do you think are most important in a good manager?

20. Why do you think you're the best person for this job?

Christi Braden

Christi used one of those little cameras that sat on top of her computer. She loved to go on-line and chat with people who also had cameras on their computers. She said using the live video added a whole new dimension to her on-line conversations.

After earning a bachelor's degree in computer science, Christi had worked in the telecommunications industry for two years. We worked with her on her career plan, but what we thought was especially interesting about Christi was that she did nearly all of her networking and interviewing on-line. She said she liked it, and she thought her employers were impressed because it showed her initiative to use and embrace a newer technology. And, since her background was in computers and communications, most of the people she talked to were in related fields and were already actively using the Internet.

Christi explained, "The hardest part about live interviews is the scheduling. It's not like a newsgroup, where you can just go visit whenever you want." Christi said that a live interview required planning and organization. "Plus, the only people who will meet me on-line are people who already know me or who know of me, or people who have received a resume and are familiar with my job situation."

This setup proved to be successful for Christi. She scheduled several interviews on-line and received a great job offer as a result!

Internet Interviewing & Networking

Remember, the Internet will be an excellent resource for your job search. You never know how an employer will respond to you or how actively he or she uses the Internet, so you want to be prepared! Understand and practice your e-mail and chat room conversations. The more you use them, the better off you will be. If you are unfamiliar with these tools, you need to get on-line and start playing. Bring in your friends to talk in an Internet meeting room. Send some jokes or funny stories back and forth to your friends—just get comfortable with your time on the Internet. Believe us, communicating on the Internet is easy, fun, and very, very helpful in your job search.

Now let's look at how you can develop a *daily plan* to make your job search on the Internet a fruitful one.

Putting the Internet to Work for You Each Day

*Spiritual energy flows in and produces effects
in the phenomenal world.*

WILLIAM JAMES

WHILE READING THIS BOOK, you're preparing for a dynamic job search on the Internet. You've learned how to practice creative visualization exercises and to get in touch with your inner self. You understand the importance of knowing who you are and what your goals are before beginning your job search. You've learned how to uncover the heart and soul of your being through contemplation and creative visualization exercises. You've recognized the importance of self-affirmations and of acting "as if." You know that thoughts are things, so if you think and act as though you're already in the position you're seeking, you're already making this dream come true!

You've become aware of the importance of defining your life's mission and goals; for what good is life without a mission and purpose? How can you possibly find a job you'll love if you don't know what you want to do or what your life's mission is?

Now you've completed the exercises in creative visualization and mission setting. You've prepared your Heart & Soul resume—one for mailing, a nice presentation for face-to-face meetings, and other versions for electronic scanning and the Internet. You've researched and defined your ideal employer and generated a list of potential employers to target using the Internet. You've practiced and honed your networking skills as well as your interviewing skills. It's time to discuss your proactive plan of action, your daily Internet job search plan, which is the sixth secret—a vital, synergistic part of the whole Heart & Soul Internet job search.

HEART & SOUL TIP

Thoughts are things—they are real. So if you act and think as if you're in the position you're seeking, then you're already making this dream come true!

Remember, no dreams can come true if you don't have a concrete plan to make them real. So think of everything you must do on a daily basis, both on the Internet and off, to make your career dreams a reality.

What must you do on the Internet each day to make your job search efficient, quick, and successful? To make your dreams a reality? The following suggestions may or may not apply to your situation. Tailor them to meet your own needs. A true Heart & Soul Internet job search incorporates a comprehensive synergy of different components that all work together to help you be successful in obtaining your dream job.

HEART & SOUL TIP

No dreams can come true if you don't have a concrete plan to make them real!

Looking for work is your job now, so treat it like a job. Devote your heart and soul to this job search. As with anything in life, the more heart and soul you give to anything, the more results (gifts from life) you can expect.

1. Research different employer Web sites and submit your resume on-line to the appropriate companies.

2. Visit chat rooms or newsgroups and network on-line with both cold and warm contacts. Or e-mail someone in an appropriate company and introduce yourself. (Remember, cold contacts are individuals you don't know. Warm contacts are people you know or to whom you have been referred by a mutual friend or acquaintance.)

3. Research the resume/job databases on the Internet. Post your resume at the appropriate sites.

4. Check the home pages of major search engines for new resources. Remember, the more research you do, the better equipped you are when looking for a job.

5. Go back to your favorite discussion groups and locate some new ones that are relevant to your areas of interest. This is a great way to network with others.

6. Write down your "to do" list and review your daily Internet checklist periodically to ensure that you're doing everything possible to get that dream job. Add new "to do" items as you progress in your job search. Keep detailed notes of all your contacts and information. Be organized.

At the end of the day, do something you love. Surrender your worries. Do something simply for the pure joy of doing it. This is the time to take your focus off your Internet job search and relax and recharge those inner Heart & Soul batteries. Take a walk in a park or forest and breathe in the beauty of the trees. Put on a favorite CD or cassette and listen to some music. Plunge into a bubble bath or hot tub and relish in the bubbles. Be creative about your own activities. We're sure that you have many wonderful hobbies that are great stress-busters, so now's the time to enjoy them!

HEART & SOUL TIP

At the end of the day, take a break! Enjoy the rest of the day.

Always Check the Home Pages of the Major Search Engines

The Lycos, InfoSeek, Yahoo!, and Excite search engines, to name a few, all catalogue and reference career Web sites, newsgroups, chat lines, and articles and information that will help you in your Internet job search. The information on the Internet is changing rapidly, and you need to regularly visit these central sites to keep up-to-date on the latest career resources available. Just as watching the daily news on TV and reading the daily newspaper keep you abreast of current events, so will visiting the career Web sites daily. This simple activity will keep you in the know.

HEART & SOUL TIP

Visiting career Web sites daily will keep you informed of any changes.

Your Daily Plan Quick-Glance Checklist

The greatest difficulty in implementing a successful daily plan lies in your ability to effectively manage your time throughout your entire job search process, especially if you already have a full-time job. It is vital that you are organized so that you can successfully manage your time. If organization is a problem for you, you can practice organizational strategies each day to help strengthen this skill so that you can accomplish everything you need to do each day.

In Table 6.1 (page 122) we have put together a checklist that you can use or revise to fit your particular situation. It will help you become better organized. It is similar to the daily Internet job search plan that we illustrated earlier in this chapter, but is designed as a "quick-glance" checklist that you can scan each morning and periodically throughout the day. Post this or one like it on your refrigerator or on a bulletin board above your desk.

Every Morning

- Practice creative visualization exercises and visualize yourself in your new job. Practice affirmations and act as if you already have the job.
- Review your mission, objectives, goals, dreams, and daily (functional) strategies.
- Venture out on the Internet—go on-line.

Throughout the Day—Daily Internet Job Search Plan

- Research 10 target employer Web sites and submit your resume.
- Network on-line with ten cold and ten warm contacts.
- Research and recheck 10 resume/job databases on the Internet.
- Check the home page of at least one major search engine for new resources.
- Participate in your favorite (and find new) discussion groups.
- Check and respond to e-mail messages that result from your networking.
- Visit your favorite chat lines or search for new ones for possible networking opportunities.
- Visit your favorite (and search for new) career Web sites.
- Make lists with new ideas for the next day's on-line job search activities.

Non-Internet—Off-line

- Network with companies and individuals that work off-line.
- Check your favorite newspapers and trade magazines for job openings.
- Send all the necessary thank-you letters and follow-up letters in addition to resumes and cover letters.

End of Day

- Take a break. Surrender your worries and do something you love. Enjoy the moment. Sit on your patio or front porch and watch the sun go down or take your dog for a walk.

■ **TABLE 6.1**
Heart & Soul Daily Job Search Quick-Glance Checklist

A Reminder—Nourish Your Heart and Soul Throughout Your Job Search

We mentioned creative visualization exercises in Chapter 2 and earlier in this chapter. Creative visualization is so important to the Heart & Soul philosophy that we're reemphasizing it here.

Each day set aside some time to do creative visualization exercises. It's best to schedule a specific time each day to do these exercises and get in a regular routine. The best time is either after you get up in the morning or just before you go to bed at night. Through creative visualization, you can get in touch with your inner self (your heart and soul). During this time, reaffirm your mission and your vision of how you're going to find your dream job on the Internet. These exercises help you to not lose sight of your goals and your heart's dreams. They are the intrinsic foundation of the Heart & Soul proactive Internet job search plan.

HEART & SOUL TIP

Don't forget to include traditional "non-Internet" activities in your proactive job search plan: creative visualization, discipline, focus, awareness, and preparedness.

Another way to nourish your heart and soul is to review your list of goals and activities that will help you in your mission. Review them, rewrite them, change them, and add to them each day.

On an ongoing basis, check your "discipline muscles." Are you living in the moment? Are you staying focused? Are you aware of what's needed for that day? Are you organized and prepared for interviews and job search activities? Discipline, focus, awareness, and preparedness are all vital components of your daily Internet plan of action.

When your job-searching day is done, relax and enjoy yourself.

All of these steps are very important. Too often, people become so wrapped up in looking for jobs that they forget how to relax. They lose faith in their dreams. Don't let the job search woes get the best of you. With each test, you will become stronger. Even during downtimes when money problems are a concern, or when you are worried about your future, take heart! Things will get better because you are doing all the right things!

HEART & SOUL TIP

Never give up your dreams and goals. People who give up never succeed!

The following story illustrates how we helped one of our candidates, Elizabeth Anderson, with her Heart & Soul Internet job search plan.

Elizabeth Anderson

Elizabeth e-mailed us a copy of her resume with the message "HELP!" She then telephoned us and said, "I'm depressed. I'm so tired of hearing that I'm overqualified for all the positions I'm applying for. To hear that I'm overqualified isn't very comforting at all! I need a job!"

Elizabeth had been a casting director for major motion pictures as well as television shows and commercials. She had also been actively involved in volunteering for numerous community organizations, and had even worked as a sales consultant for an upscale aromatherapy company. She had so many talents that she simply couldn't focus on one career. We encouraged Elizabeth to spend at least 20 minutes a day doing creative visualization exercises, which she happily agreed to do. We worked closely with her on defining her mission and setting objectives, one of which was to find a good job! She confirmed that she wanted to continue in the entertainment industry, but in such a competitive and tight field, she needed some assistance in her actual job search.

Elizabeth hadn't been using a real resume. She had simply been distributing a list of movie and commercial credits, which didn't contain much selling power. Figure 6.1 (pages 124–127) shows the Heart & Soul resume we wrote for Elizabeth. Of course, we made a text file and a scannable version of her resume. In addition, we helped her create a multimedia resume that we posted on her personal Web site. This was perfect for her because she was involved in many high-profile movies and entertainment-related projects.

■ **FIGURE 6.1**
Elizabeth Anderson's Brochure Resume (Cover Sheet)

HEART & SOUL TIP

We prepared a brochure-style resume for Elizabeth. This is the cover sheet.

ELIZABETH ANDERSON

Professional Casting Director

603 Anywhere Street
City, State 10000
Phone Number
eliza@saltwatersx.com
www.saltwatersx.com

■ **FIGURE 6.1**
Elizabeth Anderson's Brochure Resume (Page 1)

ELIZABETH ANDERSON
603 Anywhere Street
City, State 10000
Phone Number
eliza@saltwatersx.com
www.saltwatersx.com

Executive Profile

Dynamic, creative, and multitalented Executive & Consultant in the entertainment industry with an expansive background in Project Management, Casting Management, Entrepreneurial Endeavors, Marketing and Promotions, and Entertainment Artist Relations. Consistently successful in developing, organizing, and initiating start-up offices and businesses. In-depth background building and nurturing client relationships with actors, producers, directors, agents, celebrities, and studios. Thorough understanding of film and television production as well as multimedia and interactive markets including CGI (computer graphics and animation). Instrumental in developing and promoting the careers of actors as a result of artful casting and direction. Strong management qualifications with comprehensive experience in all aspects of marketing and promotions, actor relations, budget management, personnel, and contract negotiations. Expertise developed in SAG/AFTRA union negotiations.

Ability to develop and build business operations to maximize growth and profitability. Skilled executive liaison and public speaker with domestic and international experience. Proactive leader, motivator, and negotiator. Excellent time management and organizational skills with ability to prioritize responsibilities and manage multiple projects simultaneously.

Empowered, self-focused, and self-directed professional who thoroughly enjoys a creative environment that provides innovative challenges. Desire a leadership position that will offer rewarding opportunities in the entertainment industry and provide an avenue to significantly contribute to a company's efficiency, organization, growth, and profitability.

EDUCATION
Bachelor of Arts in Metaphysical Studies & Parapsychology
Minor: Psychology
University of New York, New York, New York

Music & Voice
Juilliard School of Music, New York, New York

COMPUTER OPERATIONS
Windows 3.1, Window 95, Microsoft Word, MS Publisher, Netscape, PC & Macintosh

Entertainment Industry Experience

Producer & Multimedia Consultant, Casting Director
"DEVIL'S ISLAND" CD-ROM PROJECT, Santa Monica, California, 1995 to Present

- *Casting Director:* Responsible for casting live action, voice and virtual, for "Devil's Island," an on-line CD-ROM MUD (multi-user domain), available on the market in 1999.

- *Entertainment Industry Relations:* As a Consultant, Producer, and Casting Director, continuously build and nurture a strong network of associates in the entertainment industry as a result of providing superior service and excellent communication skills. Interact extensively with actors to develop long-term career goals and work with talent on special projects including "Devil's Island" to create lifelike artificial intelligence.

- *Scripting:* Responsible for working and collaborating with improvisational actors to create and write realistic scenes and scripts for CD-ROM project.

- *Communications Liaison & Mediator:* Liaison between creative, technological, and production personnel. Responsible for serving as mediator between actors, directors, studios, and agents. Ability to communicate complex technology, designs, and plans utilized in production to diverse industry personnel.

- *Contracts & Negotiations:* Offer consulting services to actors and entertainment professionals to provide information regarding contracts and legal issues.

- *Advertising & Marketing:* Conceptualize, create, and implement innovative advertising and marketing strategies to generate revenue, promote products, expand business, and increase profitability. Work with other companies to develop co-op advertising plans to promote interrelated products.

- *Budget Management:* Review, analyze, and administer budget for operating expenditures on special projects. Responsible for financial performance analysis and business planning/development functions.

Casting Director
ELIZABETH ANDERSON CONSULTING, Santa Monica, California, 1992 to Present
NORTHERN CASTING, San Francisco, California, 1986 to 1987

- *Casting Management:* As owner of company, manage and direct overall casting operations and responsible for casting talent and extras in film, television, and commercial projects. Notable projects have included Shapiro Productions, MCI, Pepsi, AT&T, and Toyota television commercials; *The Tenderloin*, an independent feature film directed by Alexa Tenia; *A Knight's Tale*, AFI Final Year project directed by Peter Tanner and supervised by producer Eddie Hanson.

- *Auditions:* Recruit, interview, and audition talent for broadcast projects. Devise categories for talents' resumes and entertainment profile sheets, which include head shots and bios. Responsible for organizing and briefing talent concerning scheduling of production and daily call sheets.

- *Talent Files:* Update and manage files, compiling lists of talent, schedules, and pertinent information needed for future projects.

- *Entertainment Industry Relations:* On an ongoing basis, responsible for the development/nurturance of entertainment industry relationships. Coordinate activities and assignments of booked talent, which involves in-depth communication and organization between actors, directors, and studios.

- *Contract Negotiations:* Arrange and negotiate contracts and fees for actors. Review contracts to ensure the implementation of special requests and concerns.

■ **FIGURE 6.1**
Elizabeth Anderson's Brochure Resume (Page 3)

Entertainment Industry Experience

Associate Casting Director, Assistant & Consultant
Dianne Dawson, Los Angeles, California, 1989 to 1990
Tim Mikaels, Los Angeles, California, 1988 to 1989
Abe Donavon, Los Angeles, California, 1989
Carol Tineman, Los Angeles, California, 1987 to 1988

■ *Casting Management:* Assisted in managing overall casting operations for Dianne Dawson and other professionals listed above.

■ *Office Development:* Organized and set up casting offices, which included coordinating files, compiling lists of talent, scheduling, and booking. Recruited, interviewed, and auditioned talent for broadcast projects. Developed categories for talents' resumes and entertainment profile sheets, head shots, and bios.

■ *Film, Broadcast & Commercial Projects:* Assisted in casting actors in the following projects: *City Slickers,* feature film, Castle Rock Pictures, directed by Ron Benson; *Career Opportunities,* feature film, Universal Pictures, directed by Steven Stenson; *The Girl Who Came Between,* NBC MOW, Saban/Sherick Productions, directed by Marvin Menton; and *A Quiet Little Neighborhood, A Perfect Little Murder,* Hoffman/Israel Production, NBC MOW, directed by Tina Daniels.

■ *Consultant:* During this time, served as a consultant for the following projects: *Blood Ties,* pilot, Fox TV; two Gale Anne Hurd projects, including one feature and one HBO MOW; *Lovecraft,* Samuel Goldwyn, feature; and *Freejack* and *Morgan Creek,* features, Carrie Townes.

■ *Associate Casting Director to Lou Diagaimo:* Assisted in all casting operations for *The Package,* feature film directed by Andrew Davis, and *The Guardian,* feature film directed by Bob Daly.

■ *Casting Assistant to Susan Bluestein:* Assisted in all casting operations for Tri Star Pictures, which included *Onassis,* 4-hr. mini-series, ABC; *Something Is Out There,* 4-hr. pilot/series opening, NBC; *Red Earth, White Earth,* MOW CBS; and *Who's Harry Crumb?* feature film, Tri Star.

Agent
MIGHTY TALENT
San Francisco, California, 1985 to 1986

■ *Department Development:* Responsible for developing and initiating an Adult Division for this talent agency. Also in charge of spearheading the development of a successful Comedy Division.

■ *Account Management:* In charge of managing major accounts including Ketchum and Saatchi & Saatchi.

After we had completed Elizabeth's main Heart & Soul resume, along with all the different versions she needed, we plunged on-line with her and helped her find a target list of employers. We encouraged her to commit to her own daily Internet job search plan (identical to the sample in this chapter) for four weeks. If she didn't generate any interviews or positive activity in that span of time, then we promised to reevaluate and problem-solve her situation.

Elizabeth had already been practicing creative visualization and affirmations, so we didn't have to coach her in these areas. She mailed her brochure resume and cover letter to each target employer. Then she incorporated the daily Internet job search plan into her routine activities. She pursued the Internet aggressively, and within two weeks she had obtained five great leads, two of which turned into good interviews and one that turned into an acceptable job offer—all from the Internet! She also received three good leads from the resumes she had mailed traditionally. She felt confident that she could generate more activity in the following weeks because she still had more target employers and networking contacts to follow up with. She chose, however, to accept the offer she had on the table from one of the companies she found on the Internet because it was a generous offer and was directly in line with her career goals, mission, and dreams. Case closed!

Winning Interviews and Job Offers

*You've got to believe deep inside yourself that
you're destined to do great things.*

JOE PATERNO, 1926

MARKETING IS NOT REALLY a secret. Everyone knows that you have to successfully market yourself to find a good job. Thoroughly understanding how to market yourself on the Internet is the seventh secret to the Heart & Soul Internet job search. Remember, implementing a Heart & Soul marketing plan for the Internet is as important as getting on the Internet in the first place!

Our synergistic Heart & Soul approach to helping you in your job search means that you must utilize all methods when looking for a job. With this in mind, remember that it's important to use the Internet as *one* of the vital tools in your job search. Don't depend on it as the only source for finding a job.

1. Motivate employers and colleagues to help you by networking on-line.

2. Target company Web sites to find the best job.

3. Power up with the power of newsgroups/USENET.

4. Ride the new wave of Internet chat lines.

5. Market with e-mail.

■ **TABLE 7.1**
Internet Marketing Strategies

HEART & SOUL TIP

Capitalizing on the Internet to supplement and enhance your job search is a powerful career tool that can be successful and rewarding.

Relying solely on the Internet for your job search is a mistake; however, capitalizing on the Internet to supplement and enhance your job search by networking and effectively marketing yourself is a powerful career tool that can be successful and rewarding. Table 7.1 lists five marketing strategies to help you in your Heart & Soul Internet job search. See Chapter 5 for more information.

Tommy Adams

Tommy Adams was unhappy in his job as a sales and business consultant with a small new company called Response Technology Managers. He had thought it might be a good opportunity, but now, after only one year, he was sure he had made a mistake. The job was mostly about sales, and Tommy didn't like sales. He wasn't sure what he wanted to do, and this was the problem. He had been out of college for three years and had already had three jobs, but none of them had satisfied him. He kept thinking that there must be something better. With a master's degree in business administration, he should be able to find a good career job. But, in his heart of hearts, Tommy just didn't know what would make him happy.

Tommy had been frantically searching the classifieds every Sunday to find a good job. He had continued using the resume he had prepared while in college, but worried that it wasn't powerful enough. In fact, he worried about his own self-worth. Did he have any talents at all? Was he doomed to stay in this job that stifled him and seemed to be leading nowhere? Tommy knew he needed help.

When Tommy walked in our door, he seemed to have all the confidence in the world. However, after we talked to him a while, we realized that his self-esteem was really suffering. He worked in a high-pressure environment that he didn't like. The more miserable he became, the more his self-esteem suffered;

and the longer he stayed in that environment, the more confused he became about what he wanted to do. We knew that his job search was going to be challenging.

"What have you been doing to find a job?" we asked.

"Well, I've been going through the Sunday classifieds, of course," he said, "and I've been thinking about getting on the Internet. I've heard that is a good way to find a job."

We explained that, yes, the Internet is a great way to find a job, but only if you approach it in the right way. Our Heart & Soul Internet job search involves much more than just jumping on the Web. We described the whole Heart & Soul process to him.

He had been searching for a job for more than six months and had had only one interview. When we looked at his resume, we understood why he wasn't getting more. He needed a much more in-depth, powerful resume at this point in his career. It was crucial that he have this before going on the Internet.

HEART & SOUL TIP

A working environment that doesn't match your personality or career goals will stifle you and kill your spirit. It can damage your self-esteem and cloud your vision with false images about yourself.

But before he could have a true Heart & Soul resume, he had to focus on a career. To help him, we administered our career planning and focus series, which includes the *Strong Interest Inventory* and the *Myers-Briggs Type Indicator*. After analyzing these results during several sessions with Tommy, he had an epiphany! He loved computer technology and problem solving! He was delighted when he discovered that a job as a management consultant with a large company would be perfect for him.

"I can't believe I haven't thought of this before," Tommy told us. "After all, I've always loved tinkering around with computers. Plus, I enjoy designing systems and programs to streamline operations. At my present job, that's what I love to do. I don't like the sales part, but I like all the computer stuff."

Tommy glowed when he realized that he could find a job that would make him happy. We then explained how he could use creative visualization to see himself in that new job. We defined how it was important to visualize and define his mission, then set goals to work toward his mission. Tommy wrote down his mission for the first time: "To become the best management consultant in the world." He would achieve this mission by solving problems as a company's information systems manager. After this, Tommy created a career map that outlined the steps to achieve his objectives. His first short-term goal was to obtain a job as a management consultant with a reputable technological company. Now that his career plan was in place, the next big focus was marketing. Tommy had to make sure his marketing materials were up to par.

Following is Tommy's old resume (see Figure 7.1, page 132). Notice that it's not a very effective marketing tool. Next is the power resume that we prepared for him, which became his own marketing brochure (see Figure 7.2, pages 133–135). This brochure style of resume has been consistently successful in landing interviews for our clients.

■ **FIGURE 7.1**
Tommy Adams's "Before" Resume

Tommy Adams
1505 Anywhere Street, City, State 10000
Phone Number - E-mail: tommy@saltwater.com

Experience 1997 to Present	Response Technology Managers, Nashville, TN <u>Sales and Business Consultant</u> Develop marketing literature and product pricing for sales proposals. Contract for the development of interactive voice response technology. Present quality of care measurement solutions to physician management groups.
1996 to 1997	Intersystems, Nashville, TN <u>Territory Representative</u> Developed relationships with existing customer base. Managed the growth of value-added resellers. Consulted prospective customers about interactive voice response technology.
Summer 1995	The Atlantic Group, Nashville, TN <u>Marketing Services Assistant</u> Developed client base of professionals in healthcare. Assimilated customer satisfaction data into graphics for marketing promotion in Mississippi. Downloaded new access to Medicaid database information and provided on-site training for users in Kentucky and Ohio. Resolved account problems in Kentucky and Ohio.
1991 to 1995	Clemson Football Program, Clemson, South Carolina Student Equipment Manager Prepared equipment for practices, scrimmages and games.
EDUCATION	Clemson University, Clemson, South Carolina Master of Business Administration, 1996 Marketing and Management Information Systems GPA: 3.64 Accelerated BA/MBA Program Completed coursework in Market Research, Customer Satisfaction Theory, Buyer Behavior, Strategy, Decision Support Systems, and Telecommunications. Clemson University, Clemson, South Carolina Bachelor of Arts, 1995 Economics Major GPA: 3.62 Graduated <u>Magna Cum Laude</u>

■ **FIGURE 7.2**
Tommy Adams's "After " Resume (Cover Sheet)

TOMMY ADAMS

A Presentation
of
Professional Credentials

1505 Anywhere Street
City, State 10000
Phone Number
tommy@saltwater.com

■ **FIGURE 7.2**
Tommy Adams's "After" Resume (Page 1)

TOMMY ADAMS
1505 Anywhere Street
City, State 10000
Phone Number
tommy@saltwater.com

Professional Objective & Profile

Results-oriented, diverse **Business Consultant** with more than seven years of experience encompassing positions in *Consulting, Sales, Marketing, and Management.* Excellent problem-solving and analytical skills with experience analyzing and evaluating information systems and applications. Extremely resourceful with strong interest in high-intensity training in Information Technology (IT) and Change Integration (CI) services, including programming and design. Familiar with Information Systems, products and services. Skilled in planning, developing, and implementing systems to streamline operations and increase efficiency. Proficient in Microsoft Word, Excel, PowerPoint, Access, Oracle, and SPSS.

Strong interpersonal skills with ability to effectively interact with all types of individuals and all levels of management and personnel. Committed to providing superior service in the most demanding business environments to clients, with ability to build and nurture client relationships. Proactive leader with experience in training and development. Also, skilled in marketing and advertising with experience in designing, developing, and producing a diversity of marketing materials targeted to professional markets. More than five years of Spanish.

Desire a challenging position as a **Management Consultant** that offers international exposure, ongoing training, and career opportunities to build an excellent consulting career.

EDUCATION
Master of Business Administration
Management Information Systems & Marketing
Bert Graduate School of Management at Clemson University, Clemson, South Carolina, 1996
GPA: 3.6/4.0

- Accelerated BA/MBA Program
- Concentration in Strategy, Decision Support Systems & Telecommunications
- Financed 100% of education through employment and academic scholarships

Bachelor of Arts
Major in Economics
Clemson University, Clemson, South Carolina, 1995
GPA: 3.62/4.0 - Graduated Magna Cum Laude

- Elected into the Clemson Honor Scholars Program
- Awarded Clemson University's Top-Ten Academic Scholarship
- Awarded South Carolina Academic Scholarship
- Elected Scholarship Chairman of Phi Kappa Psi fraternity

■ **FIGURE 7.2**
Tommy Adams's "After" Resume (Page 2)

Professional Experience

Sales & Business Consultant
RESPONSE TECHNOLOGY MANAGERS, Nashville, Tennessee, 1997 to Present

■ *Company Organization:* Recruited to spearhead the planning, development, and implementation of company's systems, policies, and procedures. On a continuing basis, evaluate, analyze, plan, and develop long-range strategic business plans and organizational goals.

■ *Information Systems & Finance:* Design financial systems and cash flow models to streamline operations and increase efficiency. Utilize Excel to produce cash flow spreadsheets.

■ *Product Development & Research:* Coordinate market research activities, maintain database and competitor information, and assist with product/service development and pricing strategy.

■ *Business Planning & Marketing:* Responsible for strategic planning and development of an integrated marketing plan targeted to service-based companies including Physician Management Groups and restaurants. Wrote company's business plan and conceptualized, developed, and executed comprehensive sales and marketing campaign that included innovative marketing materials and brochures. Prepare, administer, and control budgets for marketing and advertising.

■ *Sales & Business Development:* Sell and market interactive voice response systems that are used to monitor customer service and quality control. Responsible for managing new business development and strategic planning to maximize growth and profitability. Establish growth plans for individual accounts and personally manage account calls, presentations, and contract negotiations. Negotiate contracts for software and hardware for companies and responsible for account service operations.

■ *Client Relations:* Continuously establish and maintain an exemplary network of business associates in Information Technology Services due to extensive interaction and strong communication skills.

Territory Sales Representative
INTERSYSTEMS, Nashville, Tennessee, 1996 to 1997

■ *Sales & Business Development:* Sold and marketed interactive voice response systems and applications. Responsible for selling a variety of products, including Internet products, interactive solutions, and predictive dialers. Developed business opportunities and marketing strategies to maximize growth and profitability and expand market penetration.

■ *Account Management:* Held direct responsibility for the development/nurturing of client relationships, core prospect marketing, financial analyses, competitive contract negotiations, bidding/quotes, and management of accounts. Assisted in achieving and surpassing regional sales quota of $2 million annually for company.

■ *Client Relations & Service:* Held full responsibility for developing and nurturing client relationships between major companies including Norstan, ATS, Sprint, and Williams Telecommunications. Interfaced with a variety of telecommunication companies to provide products that included Nortel and Siemens products, TBX, mainframes, switches, databases, and ACDs.

Marketing Services Assistant
The Atlantic Group, Nashville, Tennessee, Summer 1995

■ *Marketing:* Assisted in conducting marketing research activities to develop client base of healthcare professionals.

Student Equipment Manager
Clemson Football Program, Clemson, South Carolina, 1991 to 1995

■ *Management:* Assisted receivers and special teams' coaches as needed. This included managing and maintaining football equipment as needed for practices, scrimmages, and games. This position required strong organizational and management skills.

After we prepared Tommy's Heart & Soul resume, along with the text and scannable versions, we discussed how he could use the Internet to market himself. We emphasized that it was important to use all the traditional job search methods in addition to the Internet.

Tommy networked with friends, colleagues, and businesses both in the traditional sense by telephoning and setting up appointments and by using the Internet and his e-mail. He also went on-line and researched companies that interested him.

We described to Tommy the importance of marketing when planning a Heart & Soul Internet job search. He decided to use every opportunity to market himself and find the job of his dreams. With his new mission, dreams, and goals, Tommy was a changed man. He was learning how to take charge of his life and to create the kind of life he wanted. He told us that he was "energized" for the first time in several years.

The first thing Tommy did on the Internet was post an article to a newsgroup on management consulting. He understood that this was an effective marketing tool.

Subject: Management Consultant
From: Tommy Adams

Are you, or is anyone you know, looking for an outstanding, goal- and results-oriented Management Consultant in Information Systems? I am seeking a position in Nashville, Tennessee, as a Management Consultant and have a proven background in designing and implementing systems to streamline operations, positively affect quality control, and increase efficiency. I am also interested in ongoing high-intensity training programs in Information Technology, including programming and design.

Thank you very much for your assistance. I look forward to communicating with you either electronically or by phone.

Eagerly waiting to hear from a company or associate about a career opportunity as a Management Consultant,

Tommy Adams
Phone Number
tommy@saltwater.com

Almost immediately Tommy received a reply from a man who instructed him to check out the Web site for Prentiss Walker (see Figure 7.3 on pages 138–139). This man had read Tommy's message and thought he might enjoy working for this company. To illustrate a sample of what many companies post on their Web sites, we have included part of the information that Tommy found on Prentiss Walker's Web site.

Sounds like a brochure, doesn't it? Companies are definitely using the Internet to their advantage—to sell themselves to potential employees! After thoroughly researching this company's Web site, Tommy determined that he'd like to work for this company. He liked that they were looking for "analytical thinkers who want to join the technology revolution" and that they were offering "high-intensity training in all the skills to get started."

Figure 7.4 (page 140) shows the letter we prepared for Tommy to send to the company. He sent his physical resume and cover letter as a follow-up after he had already submitted his resume on-line.

Tommy won an interview with this company and obtained the job of his dreams as a management consultant. He said he knew so much about the company after researching its Web site that his interview was flawless. "People have no idea how important it is to truly know and understand their mission and dreams before they start looking for a job. I've told many of my friends that they need to find out what they really want to do. Thank goodness I didn't wait until I was near the end of my career search to get organized!"

Remember, a true Heart & Soul Internet job search incorporates synergistic, in-depth strategies to help you attain the job of your dreams. And if it's not the job of your dreams, it should be a job that's a stepping-stone leading to the job of your dreams, since not everyone is going to land the job of their dreams the first time. Sometimes it takes building your career with several jobs before you finally find that special one you've been looking for. The Heart & Soul Internet job search is a comprehensive plan that can help you discover who you are and what will make you happiest in life. If you're not doing something you love in your career, you're not going to be happy.

A vital component of the Heart & Soul Internet job search is marketing. We've outlined Internet marketing strategies to assist you. Always remember that when searching for that Heart & Soul job, you become a product that you have to market to the consumers (the potential employer and/or colleagues who can assist you). If you want to be noticed, you must know how to market yourself!

Worksheet 7.1 (page 141) provides space for you to create a personal marketing page, where you can list some innovative marketing strategies to sell yourself on the Internet. Be creative, and have fun with your ideas!

HEART & SOUL TIP

A true Heart & Soul Internet job search incorporates synergistic, in-depth strategies to help you attain the job of your dreams.

■ **FIGURE 7.3**
Example of Employer's Web Page

Prentiss Walker

CAREER OPPORTUNITIES

ENTRY-LEVEL CAREER OPPORTUNITIES IN INFORMATION TECHNOLOGY

With the best training program in the profession, a global perspective, and a new career model that leaves behind the old Big 6 "up or out" mentality, the Management Consulting arm of Prentiss Walker is recognized as one of the leading consulting firms in the world. With double-digit growth projected for the future, we are aggressively recruiting new consultants for our U.S. offices.

Entry-level Consultants join the firm in Information Technology (IT) Services and work with clients who seek superior information management.

Typical projects include:

- evaluation of current systems
- selection of new applications
- implementation of new applications, such as SAP
- managing the transition from legacy systems.

We are looking for analytical thinkers who seek to join the technology revolution. We welcome individuals from diverse academic backgrounds, and while some programming training is useful, it is not essential. What matters most is the quality of your mind and the depth of your resourcefulness, as we will provide the high-intensity training in all the skills you need to get started. Our training program, MITIS (MCS Information Technology Individual Study), provides the highest level of technical instruction needed for success in the profession.

We provide our employees with challenging careers that allow them to quickly develop solid technical, business advisory, and industry expertise with prestigious, multinational clients. International exposure, highly competitive compensation, and numerous opportunities for advancement in an energetic environment are all part of Prentiss Walker's experience. If you are interested in becoming a Prentiss Walker IT Consultant, the following pages will give you information on how to contact us.

■ **FIGURE 7.3**
Example of Employer's Web Page (continued)

CAREER OPPORTUNITIES IN MANAGEMENT SERVICES (MCS)

Information Technology (IT) Services

- Entry-Level IT Career Opportunities
- Experienced IT Career Opportunities
- MITIS (MCS Information Technology Individual Study)

Change Integration (CI) Services

- Experienced CI Career Opportunities
- Career Advancement Model
- Campus Recruiting
- MCS Offices and Recruiting Contacts
- Meet Your Future Colleagues at Prentiss Walker
- *Computer Times* Names Prentiss Walker the Best Place to Work for Information Systems Professionals
- Current Career Opportunities

Join one of the fastest-growing leaders in the consulting industry! With growth rates in the double digits, our ambitious growth plans reflect the increasing demand for our Information Technology (IT) and Change Integration (CI) services. Solving complex problems for top-tier companies, both multinational and domestic, is what our consultants do every day! Building technology infrastructure, developing global operations, and managing change are some of the challenging problems you'll face in a team environment that prizes collegiality over competition. We focus on six strategic industries: Financial Services, Products, Technology, Entertainment/Media/Communications, Petroleum, Utilities and Government.

Recognized as a leading global provider of management consulting services by our clients, competitors, and key industry influencers, PW is an exceptional place to launch or build your consulting career. Our career advancement model was recently cited in a major newspaper as one of the most innovative in the industry. Our model replaces the traditional lock-step framework that rewards longevity with a flexible approach that rewards contribution and development of critical knowledge and skills.

■ **FIGURE 7.4**
Tommy Adams's Letter to Prospective Employer

TOMMY ADAMS
1505 Anywhere Street
City, State 10000
Phone Number
tommy@saltwater.com

Today's Date

Alan Hansen
Director, Career Planning & Placement
Prentiss Walker
Management Consulting
100 Stormy Hill Road, #30
Atlanta, Georgia 30339

Dear Mr. Hansen:

Stephen Balkin suggested that I forward you a resume concerning a position as a **Management Consultant** for Prentiss Walker, which I have enclosed so you may review my background and credentials.

In addition to a Master of Business Administration degree with a concentration in Management Information Systems & Marketing from the Bert Graduate School of Management at Clemson University, I also possess more than seven years of experience encompassing positions in Consulting, Sales, Marketing, and Management. My areas of expertise and qualifications include the following:

■ Proven background in designing and implementing systems to streamline operations, positively affect quality control, and increase efficiency.

■ Strong interest in ongoing high-intensity training in Information Technology (IT) and Change Integration (CI) services, including programming and design.

■ Comprehensive overall knowledge of Information Systems and applications with proficiency in Microsoft Word, Excel, PowerPoint, Access, Oracle, and SPSS.

■ Strong analytical, organizational, and negotiation skills.

■ Talented in establishing and maintaining an exemplary network of client relationships as a result of excellent communication skills and strong a commitment to providing superior service.

■ Proven ability to define issues, propose solutions, and implement changes.

■ Demonstrated leadership, communication, and negotiation skills.

I sincerely believe that, with my experience and career aspirations, I would be an asset to your organization. I would like to request a personal interview at your earliest convenience so we can discuss how I can best contribute to your company's goals.

Thank you, Mr. Hansen, for your consideration. I look forward to speaking with you soon.

Sincerely,

Tommy Adams

Resume Enclosed

PERSONAL MARKETING STRATEGIES

■ **WORKSHEET 7.1**
Create a Personal Marketing Page

Au Revoir!

It is now time to say good-bye and to wish you heartfelt success in your Heart & Soul Internet job search and career endeavors. Remember, if you know who you are, if you are in tune with life, and if you know your mission, you can build your dreams. Nurture those dreams and keep them close. Create plans to make them come true. Take charge of your life and pursue the career that will support and complement your dreams. Only then can you fully appreciate the true power of the Internet in your current job search. This is your life. These are all things that will make you happy—that make up your heart and soul.

We wish you well, and above all, we wish you a life that you'll love!

Getting Wired

ALTHOUGH WE ASSUME THAT most people know the basics, we're also realistic about the fact that some people still need help. This appendix is for you! If any of this information is redundant, just skip it. Remember, this book is for everyone—Internet experts as well as Internet newbies.

A Brief History

Here's a brief history of the Internet. What is now called the Internet began in the 1960s as a means to connect military computers in different cities. Similarly, in the 1980s, the National Science Foundation developed a network that gave schools and universities the ability to connect to one another. Then in the 1990s several companies allowed businesses and personal computer users access to this network called the Internet. The World Wide Web (WWW) was invented to allow people on-line to view posted documents and publications from any computer. The WWW is part of the Internet and consists of all the publications, videos, and sounds stored on major computers around the world.

As you know, advances in communication technology have happened before. Remember that little innovation called the radio? When radio first became accessible to the masses, companies large and small began broadcasting their own radio shows using rooftop antennas. These businesses were considered visionaries and leaders of the twentieth century because they harnessed this exciting new technology.

As months evolved into years, the expense of operating a radio show without generating income was difficult to justify. Thankfully, a few ingenious and resourceful people organized entertaining broadcasts that included popular vaudeville acts, dramas, and news programs and actually sold advertising time to other businesses (a bold new concept). Selling this advertising time led to huge profits for these broadcasters. They learned that as long as they offered a great show, people would listen! These listeners then became a captive audience to which businesses could market their products.

That's what's happening on the Internet right now. The millions of Web sites (and career Web sites) that create the best products (or Web pages) will naturally get the most traffic. This traffic creates an audience, and an audience creates income and other exciting opportunities. Career Web sites and company Web sites with high traffic will likely recruit the best candidates.

Presently, the real trick to mastering cyberspace is to understand how and to what extent people are using it! In other words, what's the point of listing your resume on a Web site if no one will see it? Why research an on-line career site when your local newspaper will advertise more opportunities? You need to be able to intelligently decide how to make the most of your time on the Internet. It's vital to your Heart & Soul Internet job search!

If you are new to the Internet, you will need appropriate computer equipment and some basic knowledge of the tools and software required to use and explore the Internet.

Let's start with the quick-start Heart & Soul checklist in Table A-I.1 to help you understand exactly what you need to have and know before you go on-line.

Get the Right Computer

When purchasing computer equipment for use on the Internet, speed should be your greatest concern. Even with some of the fastest equipment, the Internet can still seem slow to you, so the better equipped you are, the more productive you will be in your Internet job-searching efforts.

Recognize, however, that unless you have the latest and greatest of every piece of equipment, you can't expect the Internet and your computer to be as responsive as your TV, for which you click on the remote control and immediately switch to a different channel. Although this sort of Internet speed will

1. Get the right computer.

2. Get on the Internet.

3. Use your Web browser.

4. Understand how to use Web sites.

5. Use a search engine.

6. Save your place with bookmarks.

7. Know your e-mail.

8. Use "netiquette."

9. Use the Internet as a TOOL.

■ **TABLE A-I.1**
Quick-Start Checklist

undoubtedly be available to the masses in the future, it's not there yet. Until the better technology is more readily available, you need to be prepared for slow Internet speeds.

This appendix is not designed to teach you the technical electronic workings of a computer. You don't need to know this information to conduct a successful Internet job search. All you need is a modern computer system, a good warranty, and a helpful customer service telephone number in case you have problems. Ask one of the clerks at your local or mail-order computer store to explain modems and computer equipment. They are usually very knowledgeable and technically inclined, and they can answer most of your questions. Also, if you're ready to purchase a new system, do as much research and comparative shopping as possible before you buy. When in doubt, always purchase a faster, more powerful computer than you think you'll need. Because technology is changing virtually every day, these machines can quickly become obsolete.

HEART & SOUL TIP

You don't need to worry about having the latest and greatest equipment and software. A Web page looks exactly the same no matter what modem speed you use, just as a laser-printed page looks exactly the same whether printed at 20 pages per minute or 4 pages per minute.

You might have a computer that was state-of-the-art a few years ago but is now considered slow and cumbersome. You'll have to decide whether to donate your old system to a charity (and get the tax write-off), sell it for pennies on the dollar, upgrade it for almost what it would cost to get a new system, or buy a new system.

If you're a novice computer user, don't be intimidated! Your computer is only a tool, and you don't have to know anything more about the hardware than how to turn it on. For new users, here's a simple message: don't tinker with anything until you have received at least some basic training! Try to find

HEART & SOUL TIP

Before you buy a new computer, or upgrade your existing one, try out other computers and systems that are already set up on the Internet. Never buy anything just on the word of a salesperson.

an experienced friend or reputable computer professional to help you critique your system if you want to upgrade. And if you're buying a new computer, buy one that has everything preinstalled. We recommend buying a computer with a brand name you trust, that has a long warranty, and that offers excellent customer service. When you're ready to purchase or upgrade, consider reading a consumer magazine first to help you decide among your many options. The more research and reading you can do before you buy, the better!

Get on the Internet

Assuming that your computer is already on your desk, it's time to get on the Internet. But before you can log on, you need to sign up with an Internet service provider (ISP), such as America Online (AOL), Delphi, or Microsoft Network, to name a few. (For a list of ISPs, see Appendix II.) An ISP lets you access e-mail and the Internet for a monthly fee. Each ISP will offer value in subtly different ways. If you buy a new computer, several ISPs will probably be preloaded. Or you can visit your local computer store or, even easier, just watch for information in the mail. ISPs are in intense competition for your business, so you usually don't have to go far to find them—they're out there looking for you! You dial your ISP (via your modem) to gain access to e-mail and the Internet (or World Wide Web). Also, most ISPs allow you to communicate in other electronic forums, such as chat lines and newsgroups (as covered earlier in this book).

Because of the multitude of available ISPs, many will offer trial periods to test their service for free. You can use this free trial period to see whether you like the service. If you don't know which one to try first, ask your friends what they use—that's always a good place to start. For more information, check out the latest Internet magazines or visit your local computer store. Some ISPs let you try out their service before you load the software and register for a trial period. Millions of people, community libraries, copy and print centers, and businesses are on the Internet now; you shouldn't have a problem finding a place to go surfing on-line for free or for a nominal fee.

Use a Browser

No matter which ISP you choose, you should be able to use whatever browser you want. Your Web browser is the software that transmits the code posted on the Internet into an attractive graphic interface on your computer screen. A Web browser is simply a tool that's used to view information on the Web.

Common browsers include Netscape Navigator and Microsoft Internet Explorer; a browser will probably be provided with your ISP account. Netscape Navigator is available for computers running under many different operating systems, including OS/2, Macintosh, Windows, and UNIX, and it is available in more than 10 different languages. Microsoft Internet Explorer is one of the most popular Web browsers. It's very convenient to use because it was created by the same company that created the Windows operating systems. Whichever one you use is your personal preference. And remember, if you're not happy with one, try another.

Understand How to Use Web Sites

Getting to Web sites is really fun and easy. It involves nothing more than clicking the mouse or typing in a Web site address.

Let's explore what a Web site address is and what it means. Each Web page or site has an address known as the Uniform Resource Locator (URL) and begins with the letters "**http://**" (this stands for Hypertext Transfer Protocol, which is the protocol used to transfer information on the Web). Following this are the initials "**www**," for World Wide Web. Next is the site's domain name (the server computer that "hosts" the site) followed by an extension that identifies the entity as a commercial business (.com), organization (.org), government office (.gov), or educational institution (.edu). With a few exceptions, this is the naming format of the Web sites you will visit. For example, our publisher's Web site is located at **http://www.cpp-db.com**. The domain name is **cpp-db**, which stands for Consulting Psychologists Press and Davies-Black Publishing, and the **.com** tells you that this is a commercial business.

Microsoft Internet Explorer allows you to go to a specific Web site by clicking the "File" menu, clicking "Open," and then typing in your target Web site URL. Consult your browser's "Help" menu for more information on going directly to a Web site. The fastest and easiest way to visit a Web site is to type in its address—its URL.

Because the domain name is the only part of a Web site address that changes from company to company, most national and international corporations are easy to locate on the Web. If you want to go to a major company's Web site, type in the company's name as the domain name, plus **.com.** It doesn't always work, but if the company is big enough, don't even waste your time on the search directories! Check out the URLs of these big-name companies:

Microsoft	http://www.microsoft.com
MTV	http://www.mtv.com
JCPenney	http://www.jcpenney.com
Kodak	http://www.kodak.com

If the company's site doesn't show up right away, quit trying. Some companies use some permutation of their company letters or a company slogan as their URL. With these companies, you can use a search engine to locate their site.

Most Web sites begin with a main page, or home page, that leads to multiple pages, each with its own address defined by extensions to the main home page address. (Don't worry about what the extra extensions mean.) You need to know only that to access a Web site directly, you must type in the correct URL. All spacing, slashes, letters, and periods must be entered exactly, or you won't be able to open the company's Web site. (Keep in mind that even if you don't know the exact URL, you can always search for it via your ISP's search engine, as discussed in the next section.)

On a Web site, your mouse will take you wherever you need to go. Web site designers allow you to simply click your mouse as the cursor passes over special words, phrases, or pictures to jump or link to a different Web page.

For example, if this book page were a Web page, we could use **About the Authors**—in this different-looking font—to tell you that you can click on these words, called hypertext, to jump to a new Web site about the authors. But hypertext doesn't have to be words, or text. When clicked, many of the graphics and icons included on a typical Web page will also transport you to another Web page or site. By moving from one Web site to another, you can narrow a very broad job search down to a few specific possibilities in a matter of minutes. After a bit of practice, you'll become more and more comfortable with this kind of electronic on-line travel. It's really fun!

What Is a "Hit" on a Web Site?

HEART & SOUL TIP

A "hit" happens every time someone visits a Web site. Many sites track how many hits they get each day, week, and month. This helps companies sell advertising and track their Web site usage.

For career Web sites, traffic, or "hits," offers the greatest way for companies to measure their success. Obviously, the more people that visit a company's site, the more popular the company becomes. You might have noticed that many companies are bending over backwards using audio and video clips and other interesting images to get your attention and approval. They know that at this moment, market share (the number of hits) is just as important as, if not more important than, the company's present profitability. They are fully confident that if they get the market share and attention now, big profitability will result as they attract more customers. And they're right, of course.

Use a Search Engine

With millions and millions of Web sites, how can you find the one or two that will make a difference in your job search if you don't already know the address? You need some help in finding the Web sites you want. That's where the *search engine* comes in.

A search engine is a great little helper that catalogs the Web and searches every registered Web site that contains a word or phrase that you're looking for. To locate the search directories, go to your browser and find the button or section that says "Search" or "Search the Net."

After the Search window or area opens, type **Jobs Overseas** in the Search field. Wait a few seconds, and you'll see a list of Web sites that you can visit. In some form or another, each of these Web sites incorporates the words *Jobs Overseas* in its content or title. You might locate one site entitled *How to Find Jobs Overseas* and another that reads *A Study of Labor Unions and Jobs Overseas.* Generally, the Web sites that are a closer and more accurate match to your search criteria (the words you typed) will be ranked at the top of the list. Using a search engine to explore a broad category such as *Careers* will likely turn up thousands of Web site URLs, but only about 10 of these Web site listings will be visible at a particular time. You can usually click a "Next" button or scroll down the page to find more site listings.

Some search engines offer a list of categories from which you can search, such as *Sports, Health, Careers, Travel,* etc. When you click on *Careers,* for example, a subset of options, such as *Career Advice, Employment Agencies, Headhunters and Recruiters, Companies,* will appear.

Will the Best Search Engine Please Stand Up?

There is probably no "best" search engine. You'll notice that several search engine options are available for use, including Yahoo, Excite, Alta Vista, Lycos, and InfoSeek, to name a few. (A longer list of search directories can be found in Appendix II.)

Each of these search directories searches the Web in a slightly different way, which can sometimes produce different results. These differences are beyond the scope of this book, but you should be aware that not all search engines work exactly the same way. To test them out yourself, conduct searches using the same phrase on a couple of different search engines. See if (and to what extent) the results differ between search engines.

Advertising with Hypertext

Another way for a Web site (company or individual) to capture your attention, and probably the most common among the more reputable organizations, is to use a banner advertisement. This advertisement is generated like a headline across your computer screen whenever you search for a certain word or phrase, like "Careers" or "Job Opportunities."

The search engine will still list the matches to your search, but the matches will be in text form and not as attractive as the banner ad. Often the banner ad is a very effective and powerful way to reach an audience because it is designed to attract attention. It appears only when someone is searching for similar topics, and it's easy for people to use (you click on the ad, and you're whisked off to the company's Web site). So as you enter your searches, consider visiting the banner ads that appear in addition to the matched listings.

Practice a few Internet searches. Try using a descriptive phrase like "Deforestation in South America." Or type in your favorite movie star's name and see how many (if any) Web sites are dedicated to him or her. The search engine will find the Web pages that contain those keywords. It won't take you long to get comfortable searching the Internet because it's really simple and easy. It's a fun way to travel anywhere in the world! Practice, as with anything, will make you feel more comfortable when you do your actual on-line job search.

Searching for an Employer

Many times you won't know the Web address of an employer that you are researching. That's O.K.! Just do a search. Searches are invaluable tools that help you find employers' Web sites when you know only the company name and not its URL.

Save Your Place with Bookmarks

Each browser comes with a menu item or folder called *Favorite* or *Bookmark.* Whenever you reach a Web site that you know you want to consult regularly, mark that site as a favorite or bookmark. This feature allows you to store in a file the addresses of Web pages you visit frequently. It's much faster and more convenient than starting a site search from scratch. If your chosen site is marked as a favorite or bookmark, you will save time by not having to retrace your steps through the maze of other Web sites or reenter the URL each time you want to visit a certain site.

Know Your E-mail

Your ISP will provide information on your e-mail. E-mail skills are very important for you to understand and master. In fact, e-mail is probably the single most important way people use the Internet. You need to learn the following e-mail skills to make the most of your Internet job search:

1. Send an e-mail message to a new recipient.
2. Send an e-mail message to someone already on your recipient list.
3. Add a name and e-mail address to your recipient list.
4. Receive and view e-mail messages sent to your In box.

5. View all messages you have already sent or those you've scheduled to send in your Out box.

6. Delete e-mail from your In box or Out box.

7. Attach a file (such as your resume) to an e-mail message.

8. Send one e-mail message to several people at once.

9. Send a copy of an e-mail message to a recipient in addition to your main addressee (cc:, or carbon copy).

Use "Netiquette"

Before you venture out onto the Information Superhighway, keep in mind that this is a job search and you are approaching real employers. And yes, there are certain Internet manners—a proper "Netiquette" that you need to incorporate while using the Web. We have outlined some basic Heart & Soul tips for professionalism, respect, politeness, and "Netiquette" while communicating to others on the Internet.

1. Never write in all capital letters. It's like screaming on the Internet.

2. Write complete, grammatically correct sentences.

3. Do not use slang, clichés, or informal language.

4. Treat your message recipients with respect and professionalism.

Remember, these are only general guidelines. Each newsgroup, e-mail mailing list, and chat line might have its own set of rules. It is up to you to communicate within the parameters of each individual group. Most will provide a FAQ (frequently asked questions) sheet that will orient you to their particular mission and style.

Use the Internet as a Tool

We have worked with some people who actually revere and idolize the Internet: it's big, it's powerful—an awesome giant universe. Some people are so in awe of the Web that they fear it a little. They believe that there is no better way to communicate or exchange information. Although this may be true, the Internet is still in a growth phase. Remember that it wasn't until the 1990s that companies began to offer access to home users, so that anyone with a modem and a computer could access the Internet.

HEART & SOUL TIP

Don't rely fully on the Internet in your job search! The Internet is a truly wonderful and amazing technology, but you need to incorporate your Internet job search with more traditional methods.

Is the Web the Best Way to Get a Job?

As newspapers, magazines, and other media compete for an audience, they are becoming just as aggressive as the various Web sites in helping you with your job search. Everyone is working hard to capture your attention by providing useful information or job opportunities. Although the Internet is a great way to find a job, don't depend on the Internet alone! Don't discount the old tried-and-true methods of communication and job searching. To implement a true Heart & Soul Internet job search, you must utilize all resources available to you. And remember, keep your mind open with a clear vision of what you want at all times. This is the way to truly succeed.

Stay Focused with Your Heart & Soul Discipline Muscles

Finally, it's time for you to practice venturing out into cyberspace and to understand why it's important to stay focused! Staying focused is a Heart & Soul discipline and may require strengthening those discipline muscles again and again. It's part of being aware and living in the moment. Staying focused is another element of a true Heart & Soul Internet job search.

Will Your On-line Job Search Be Like This?

You wait patiently as you log on. It always seems to take longer than it should, but you keep busy with mindless tasks while you wait—you prepare a fresh pot of coffee, flip through a few TV channels, or check to see if the mailman has come.

Finally you're connected! You open your e-mail and see that you have three messages—two are business-related and the other is a joke from a friend who attached a complete video clip that took several minutes to download. After answering each e-mail, you send a few of your own messages. After all, you know your friend will be anxious to hear what you thought of that video clip.

Now, you're ready to get busy with your job search and explore some of your favorite career Web sites. You open your Web browser and up pops a banner advertisement that says, "No More Junk Mail!" That's great, because you hate junk mail! You visit the Junk Mail Web site and see another banner advertisement that says, "Find Anyone in the United States for Free!" Your mind starts churning . . . wouldn't it be fun to locate and e-mail some friends you met in Colorado a few summers ago? Then you remember a friend in Germany and you begin to wonder what he's been doing since the last time you saw him. You find his e-mail address and write a lengthy two-page narrative on your life.

Now it's 40 minutes later, you've gulped down two cups of coffee, your hands are starting to shake from the caffeine, and you haven't even begun to pursue your Internet job search.

See how easy it is to get sidetracked on the Internet? Where's your focus? Your discipline muscles? Evidently, not where they should be!

The Web is loaded with information that can distract you from your objectives—e-mail, special programs, and information on every subject imaginable. Your best bet is to keep a notepad

HEART & SOUL TIP

Before you go on-line, make a short list of exactly what sites you want to visit and what you want to accomplish. Use your discipline muscles and don't be distracted by e-mail or other interesting Web sites. Wait until you have completed your "to do" list before you browse those other sites.

handy so you can jot down those interesting Web sites and visit them when you have free time. This requires discipline, and this is why it's important to strengthen those discipline muscles. It takes discipline to stay focused, and you're going to have to be disciplined in your Heart & Soul Internet job search if you want results.

Create a plan of specific tasks and goals to accomplish each time you go on the Internet. Learn how to focus your thoughts through creative visualization and pay attention to the job at hand. Strengthen your discipline muscles so you won't get distracted on the Internet. Be aware and stay in the moment.

Allow Extra Time for Your First On-line Visit

If you are new to the Internet, we want to encourage you to invest a few hours just getting comfortable with all the items on our quick-start checklist. When you log on, you should try to experience what it's like to move from one Web site to another. As with any type of new transportation or communication device, it takes practice to get used to it. Relax and enjoy your electronic on-line journey.

Secure Yourself with Awareness

As more people gain access to the Internet, security becomes a real issue and a potential problem. To a certain degree, many moves you make on the Web are traceable. It sounds like a "Big Brother" issue, but it doesn't have to be. We recommend that you take precautions when sending sensitive and personal information on the Web. Be aware that others might gain access to it and read it.

Security on the Net is improving each day, however. Banks, investment firms, and other sites that use your personal data are successfully doing business on-line with new and improved encoding and more secure Web browsers. These sites successfully protect all your personal data, and they'll let you know that your transactions are secure.

This appendix has introduced you to the main components of building your electronic foundation. We hope that it helps you to become familiar with topics and issues that you'll encounter once you begin your actual on-line job search. Remember, the more you practice, the better your chances for success in your Heart & Soul Internet job search.

Using Web Sites, Newsgroups, Chat Lines, and Employer Databases

ANY LISTING WE PROVIDE is not necessarily an endorsement or a recommendation. As of this writing, the numbers and addresses are correct, but of course, they are subject to change. We encourage you to critically review and compare all vendors, Web sites, ISPs, and software packages on your own as well. You might want to visit our Web site for our most up-to-date list, at **www.mindspring.com/~heartsoul**.

As you complete your Heart & Soul Internet job search, keep a written record of special newsgroups, Web sites, and chat lines that were helpful to you. When you visit our Web site, you can share your information with other Heart & Soul readers.

Mail-Order Computer Manufacturers

You'll never have any problem finding companies that want to sell you computer equipment, but following are several numbers and URLs to help you shop around for the best deal.

Dell	1-800-545-3604	www.dell.com
Gateway	1-800-424-1464	www.gateway.com
Micron	1-800-257-8361	www.micronpc.com
NEC	1-888-8-NEC-NOW	www.necnow.com
Quantex	1-800-632-5022	www.quantex.com

Mail-Order Computer Suppliers

These companies sell all kinds of computer equipment and peripherals, but they don't necessarily manufacture it.

ComputAbility	1-800-554-2186	www.computability.com
CDW	1-800-571-4239	www.cdw.com
MacWarehouse	1-800-397-8508	www.warehouse.com
MicroWarehouse	1-800-304-1934	www.warehouse.com
PC Mall	1-800-532-2292	www.pcmall.com
TigerDirect	1-800-335-4057	www.tigerdirect.com

Local Computer Trainers & Computer Dealers

These companies can be a good option if you prefer local service. Consult your Yellow Pages under "Computers."

Internet Service Providers

The following companies can provide access to the Internet. You must install their software on your computer (usually provided for free) and pay a monthly subscription fee to get Internet access and your own e-mail account. Below are some important questions you can ask while comparing each provider. When in doubt, ask a friend for a reference.

1. What are your monthly rate options and how many hours on-line do I get with each one?
2. Do I have the capability to create my own Web site?
3. What are the requirements or limitations of your Web site hosting service?
4. How and when do you bill?
5. How many phone connections do you provide for each customer?
6. What Web browser and version number comes with your package?
7. What is your cancellation policy?
8. Why should I use your service?

America Online	1-800-827-6364
AT&T Worldnet	1-800-967-5363
BellSouth	1-800-436-8638
CompuServe	1-800-848-8990

Delphi	1-800-695-4005
Earthlink	1-800-395-8425
Genie	1-800-638-9636
MCI	1-800-550-0927
Microsoft Network	1-800-386-5550
Netcom	1-800-353-6600
Prodigy	1-800-776-3449

These providers represent only a sampling of what is available. Consult your local phone book or computer shopping magazines for even more options.

Search Engines

HEART & SOUL TIP

If you ever want to find anything on the Web but are not sure where to begin, you can always use a search engine.

Search engines, or directories, are the "home base" of the Internet. These search engines provide access to information and resources available on the Internet. Many will also reference popular newsgroups, e-mail mailing lists, chat lines, company Web sites, and employment information. If you can't find the URL you need from this book or from any other resource guide, you can use any one or all of these search directories to locate a site.

Each search engine finds information and catalogues other Web sites in subtly different ways, so if you can't find what you're looking for with one search engine, try another. To access a search engine, look for a "Search" button in your Web browser. When clicked, it will allow you to gain access to any number of the following search engines:

AltaVista	NetGuide
Excite	Search.Com
Hot Bot	Snap!
InfoSeek	Web Crawler
Lycos	Yahoo
Magellan	

Employer Databases

Use the following resources to find employers and contacts in your target industry and location.

Heart & Soul Career Center   1-615-329-0300
www.mindspring.com/~heartsoul

This is the home company of the coauthors of this book (also known as ResumePLUS, Inc.). You may purchase an entire CD of data, or you may want some assistance or advice. We are here if you need us!

Dun & Bradstreet Marketplace	1-800-532-3775
www.dbisna.com	

This site offers a general employer database.

American Business Lists	1-800-555-5335
www.lookupusa.com	

This site offers a general employer database.

Career Finders Inc.	1-781-449-0312
e-mail: career@world.std.com	

This employer database specializes in career development in all industries.

CorpTech	1-617-932-3939
www.corptech.com	

This employer database specializes in high-tech companies.

TopList	1-800-347-9267
www.toplist.com	

On this site, employers are ranked by local business journals.

Select Phone	1-800-99-CD-ROM
www.procd.com	

This site offers a general employer and personal database.

Hoover's	1-800-486-8666
www.hoovers.com	

This site offers a general and specialty employer database.

Adams "Job Bank" Books
www.careercity.com

These books list prominent employers in a specific city or area.

Other Employer Database Options

- Purchase the member list of the trade association of your target industry.
- Ask your librarian for assistance and other resources.
- Look in the Yellow Pages under "Mailing Lists" for companies that sell employer data.
- Go to your local bookstore and purchase a book of "top" employers in your target area.
- Go to your local chamber of commerce and ask for the list of businesses and contacts.

Newsgroups

As of this publication, Career Mosiac catalogues many popular career-related newsgroups. Visit Career Mosaic at **www.careermosaic.com** for the most recent update or check out each one individually.

For many more listings of newsgroups and mailing lists, try **www.liszt.com** or **www.reference.com**. The latter also references Web-based forums that are analogous to newsgroups but are based on the World Wide Web. Following are some newsgroup domain names. To access one, type:

ab.jobs	fr.jobs.offres	ott.jobs
alt.building.jobs	hepnet.jobs	pa.jobs.offered
atl.jobs	houston.jobs.offered	pdaxs.jobs.clerical
au.jobs	hsv.jobs	pdaxs.jobs.computers
aus.ads.jobs	il.jobs.offered	pdaxs.jobs.construction
aus.jobs	in.jobs	pdaxs.jobs.engineering
austin.jobs	israel.jobs.offered	pdaxs.jobs.management
az.jobs	ithaca.jobs	pdaxs.jobs.sales
ba.jobs.contract	kw.jobs	pdaxs.jobs.secretary
ba.jobs.direct	la.jobs	pdaxs.jobs.temporary
ba.jobs.offered	li.jobs	pgh.jobs.offered
balt.jobs	lou.lft.jobs	phl.jobs.offered
bc.jobs	mi.jobs	qc.jobs
bermuda.jobs.offered	milw.jobs	sdnet.jobs
bionet.jobs	misc.jobs	seattle.jobs.offered
bionet.jobs.offered	misc.jobs.contract	stl.jobs
biz.jobs.offered	misc.jobs.offered	stl.jobs.offered
can.jobs	misc.jobs.offered.entry	tor.jobs
chi.jobs	nb.jobs	triangle.jobs
cmh.jobs	ne.jobs	tx.jobs
co.jobs	ne.jobs.contract	uk.jobs
comp.jobs	nj.jobs	uk.jobs.contract
comp.jobs.offered	nm.jobs	uk.jobs.offered
dc.jobs	nv.jobs	us.jobs.contract
de.markt.jobs	nyc.jobs	us.jobs.offered
dfw.jobs	nyc.jobs.contract	vegas.jobs
dod.jobs	nyc.jobs.offered	za.ads.jobs
euro.jobs	oh.jobs	
fl.jobs	ont.jobs	

Consult your ISP if you need assistance finding these newsgroups on the Web.

Career Web Sites

These career Web sites are for both individuals seeking employment and career information and employers who are recruiting for certain positions. Each site has its own unique characteristics and attributes and is very helpful to the job seeker in a unique way. We recommend that you visit each of these sites and judge it for yourself. You should always be on the lookout for additional Web sites and Internet resources that can help you in your job search. You may get some ideas from searching the Web on your profession (such as searching under "Editor" or "Programmer") or by reading the latest trade journals. Leave no stone unturned!

America's Job Bank	www.ajb.dni.us
Best Jobs USA	www.bestjobsusa.com
Career City	www.careercity.com
Career Mosaic	www.careermosaic.com
CareerBuilder	www.careerbuilder.com
CareerMagazine	www.careermag.com
CareerPath	www.careerpath.com
CareerWeb	www.cweb.com
Job Bank USA	www.jobbankusa.com
JobTrack	www.jobtrack.com
Online Career Center	www.occ.com
Passport Access	www.passportaccess.com
The Monster Board	www.monster.com
Wall Street Journal	www.careers.wsj.com
Westech Virtual Job Fair	www.vjf.com

E-mail Mailing Lists/Discussion Groups

You can join thousands of e-mail lists on the Internet, but you must find the ones that suit your specific interests and needs. Visit **www.liszt.com** or **www.reference.com** for a comprehensive listing and instructions on how to join mailing lists. These sites also provide some important dos and don'ts for Internet newbies.

Chat Lines

Chat lines are an excellent communication network on the Internet. Your ISP should provide some information about IRC (Internet relay chat). A great place to learn more about chat lines before you begin chatting is on the Web site **www.liszt.com**. Here you can also learn how to find chat groups that match your area of interest. The best way to master chat lines is to join one and just listen and talk for a while. For starters, try these channels:

#new2irc

#newuser

#newbies

#chatback

Although your chat line networking might not land you a job, you could certainly find chat groups with people with similar interests and skills as yours. Again, if you don't know or understand how to get on a chat line, consult your ISP.

Many Web sites maintain their own chat lines that you can access and participate in directly from their sites. These are fun and easy to use.

Resources

**The American Almanac of Jobs
and Salaries 1997–1998 (Serial)**
John W. Wright
Avon Books, 1996

The Art of SpeedReading People
*How to Size Up People and Speak
Their Language*
Paul D. Tieger and
Barbara Barron-Tieger
Little, Brown and Company, 1998

**To Build the Life You Want,
Create the Work You Love**
*The Spiritual Dimension of
Entrepreneuring*
Marsha Sinetar
St. Martin's Press, 1996

Chicken Soup for the Soul
Jack Canfield and
Mark Victor Hansen
Health Communications, 1993

**Connections Between Spirit &
Work in Career Development**
New Approaches and Practical Perspectives
Deborah P. Bloch and
Lee J. Richmond
Davies-Black Publishing, 1997

Cyberspace Resume Kit
*Using the Internet and World Wide Web
in Your Job Search*
Mary Nemnich and Fred E. Jandt
Jist Publishing, 1998

Dare to Win
Jack Canfield and
Mark Victor Hansen
Berkley Publishing Group, 1996

**The Directory of
Executive Recruiters 1988**
James Kennedy
Kennedy Publications, 1977

Do What You Are
*Discover the Perfect Career for You
Through the Secrets of Personality Type*
Paul D. Tieger and
Barbara Barron-Tieger
Little, Brown and Company, 1995

**Do What You Love,
the Money Will Follow**
Discovering Your Right Livelihood
Marsha Sinetar
Dell Publishing, 1989

DreamMakers
Putting Vision and Values to Work
Michele Hunt
Davies-Black Publishing, 1998

Electronic Job Search Revolution
How to Win with the New Technology
That's Reshaping Today's Job Market
Joyce Lain Kennedy and
Thomas J. Morrow
John Wiley & Sons, 1995

Heart & Soul Resumes
Seven Never-Before-Published Secrets to
Capturing Heart & Soul in Your Resume
Chuck Cochran and Donna Peerce
Davies-Black Publishing, 1998

Heart at Work
Stories and Strategies for Building Self-
Esteem and Reawakening the Soul at Work
Jack Canfield and Jacqueline Miller
McGraw-Hill, 1998

Hook Up, Get Hired!
The Internet Job Search Revolution
Joyce Lain Kennedy
John Wiley & Sons, 1995

How to Stop Worrying
and Start Living
Dale Carnegie
Pocket Books, 1985

Internet and World Wide Web
Simplified
Paul Whitehead and Ruth Maran
IDG Books Worldwide, 1997

Job Finder Series
Daniel Lauber
Planning Communications

1999 What Color Is Your Parachute?
A Practical Manual for Job-Hunters
and Career-Changers
Richard Nelson Bolles
Ten Speed Press, 1998

The Job Hunter's Spiritual
Companion
William Carver
Innisfree Press, 1998

Real People, Real Jobs
Reflecting Your Interests in the World
of Work
David H. Montross,
Zandy B. Leibowitz, and
Christopher J. Shinkman
Davies-Black Publishing, 1995

Resumes in Cyberspace
Pat Criscito, CPS, CPRW
Barrons Educational Series, 1997

The Seven Spiritual Laws of Success
A Practical Guide to the Fulfillment of
Your Dreams
Deepak Chopra
Amber-Allen Publishing, 1995

SoulWork
Finding the Work You Love, Loving
the Work You Have
Deborah P. Bloch and
Lee J. Richmond
Davies-Black Publishing, 1998

Starting Out, Starting Over
Finding the Work That's Waiting for You
Linda Peterson
Davies-Black Publishing, 1995

You Can't Afford the Luxury
of a Negative Thought
Peter McWilliams
Prelude Press, 1995

You Can Heal Your Life
Louise L. Hay
Hay House, 1987

Zen and the Art of Making a Living
A Practical Guide to Creative Career Design
Laurence G. Boldt
Penguin USA, 1993

Using the Myers-Briggs Type Indicator and the Strong Interest Inventory to Develop Your Mission and Guide Your Internet Job Search

The *Myers-Briggs Type Indicator®* (MBTI®) and the *Strong Interest Inventory®* *(Strong®)* are invaluable tools in writing a resume and cover letter with "heart and soul." By combining your values, interests, and personality (as illustrated in the MBTI and the *Strong*) with your skills and experience developed over a lifetime, along with the seven never-before-published secrets to creating a successful resume, you can transform your old resume (or a new one) into a powerful resume with real heart and soul, one that reflects you from a higher, more in-depth perspective.

Both the MBTI and the *Strong* must be administered and interpreted by a counseling professional, who not only will interpret the results of the instruments but also will discuss with you and analyze other issues in your life that are pertinent to your career and life decisions. Call a career counselor for more information. For immediate purposes, if you haven't used the MBTI or the *Strong* instrument, following are a brief history of each and some basic concepts that may help you right away when preparing a Heart & Soul resume.

History of the **Myers-Briggs Type Indicator** *(MBTI)*

The MBTI personality inventory was developed by Isabel Myers and Katharine Briggs to make Carl Jung's theory of psychological types understandable and useful in people's lives. Jung believed that many of the apparently random differences in people's behavior were actually a result of their preferred modes of perception and judgment. Perception refers to how you gather information, while judgment refers to how you come to conclusions based on what you have perceived. There are two opposite ways of perceiving, through Sensing or Intuition, and likewise two opposite ways of forming judgments, through Thinking or Feeling. Jung referred to these two pairs of opposites as the *functions.* He also described differences in the ways people prefer to focus these functions and identified another pair of opposites, which he called Extroversion and Introversion. Myers and Briggs, when constructing the MBTI instrument, added a fourth dichotomy that they thought was implicit in Jung's theory. This was the Judging and Perceiving dichotomy, which relates to one's preferences for using either one of the judging functions (Thinking or Feeling) or one of the perceiving functions (Sensing or Intuition) as the primary means of dealing with the outer world.

All of us use all eight preferences at different times. Your MBTI results indicate which of each pair of opposites you most prefer. Together, these four preferences make up what is called your *type.* Your type can be identified by the letters that are associated with your preferences on each of the four dichotomies. For example, if your type is reported as ENFP, this means you indicated preferences for Extraversion, iNtuition, Feeling, and Perceiving when you answered the MBTI items.

Table A-IV.1 summarizes the four MBTI dichotomies. Since there are two opposites for each dichotomy, there are a total of eight preferences.

The various combinations of each of the four dichotomies make up sixteen different personality types. If you don't already know your type, Table A-IV.2, "Characteristics Associated with Each Type," may help you in analyzing yours.

Please note that while the names of the MBTI preferences are familiar, in everyday use they have meanings that are different from their MBTI meanings. Remember:

- *Extravert* does not mean "talkative."
- *Introvert* does not mean "shy" or "inhibited."
- *Feeling* does not mean "emotional."
- *Judging* does not mean "judgmental."
- *Perceiving* does not mean "perceptive."

Direction of Energy

Extraversion (E)

Focus on the people and things in the outer world

Introversion (I)

Focus on the thoughts, feelings, and impressions of the inner world

Gathering Information

Sensing (S)

Focus on facts and details that can be confirmed by experience

Intuition (N)

Focus on possibilities and relationships among ideas

Making Decisions

Thinking (T)

Use impersonal, objective, logical analysis to reach conclusions

Feeling (F)

Use person-centered, subjective analysis to reach conclusions

Dealing with the Outer World

Judging (J)

Plan and organize; make decisions and come to closure

Perceiving (P)

Be spontaneous and adaptable; collect information and stay open to new options

From Introduction to Type and Careers, *Allen L. Hammer. Copyright 1993 by Consulting Psychologists Press. Reproduced with permission.*

■ **TABLE A-IV.1**
MBTI Preferences

Characteristics Associated with Each MBTI Preference

If you have not yet used the *Myers-Briggs Type Indicator* instrument, but have reviewed the above section, you may be able to identify some characteristics or preferences that apply to you. In Table A-IV.3 (page 169) we have compiled characteristics commonly associated with each MBTI preference. Read through each section and mark the characteristics that you believe strongly correlate with your personality and work ethic. Even if a particular characteristic is not in "your type," you still may have developed a certain skill or affinity for it and will want to incorporate it into your resume. Incorporate any relevant phrases into sentences that best describe you. Once you have identified a personal characteristic, think of examples and stories you may tell to illustrate it. Remember, when making a positive comment about yourself, you should always support your statement with real-life illustrations of your success. For example, don't just say, "Excellent communicator." Instead, write, "Excellent communication skills exemplified as a national workshop presenter for special industry trade shows."

	Sensing Types		Intuitive Types	
Introverts	**ISTJ** Serious, quiet, earn success by concentration and thoroughness. Practical, orderly, matter-of-fact, logical, realistic, and dependable. See to it that everything is well organized. Take responsibility. Make up their own minds as to what should be accomplished and work toward it steadily, regardless of protests or distractions.	**ISFJ** Quiet, friendly, responsible, and conscientious. Work devotedly to meet their obligations. Lend stability to any project or group. Thorough, painstaking, accurate. Their interests are usually not technical. Can be patient with necessary details. Loyal, considerate, perceptive, concerned with how other people feel.	**INFJ** Succeed by preseverance, originality, and desire to do whatever is needed or wanted. Put their best efforts into their work. Quietly forceful, conscientious, concerned for others. Respected for their firm principles. Likely to be honored and followed for their clear vision as to how to best serve the common good.	**INTJ** Have original minds and great drive for their own ideas and purposes. Have long-range vision and quickly find meaningful patterns in external events. In fields that appeal to them, they have a fine power to organize a job and carry it through. Skeptical, critical, independent, determined; have high standards of competence and performance.
	ISTP Cool onlookers—quiet, reserved, observing and analyzing life with detached curiosity and unexpected flashes of original humor. Usually interested in cause and effect, how and why mechanical things work, and organizing facts using logical principles. Excel at getting to the core of a practical problem and finding the solution.	**ISFP** Retiring, quietly friendly, sensitive, kind, modest about their abilities. Shun disagreements, do not force their opinions or values on others. Usually do not care to lead but are often loyal followers. Often relaxed about getting things done because they enjoy the present moment and do not want to spoil it by undue haste or exertion.	**INFP** Quiet observers, idealistic, loyal. Important that outer life be congruent with inner values. Curious, quick to see possibilities, often serve as catalysts to implement ideas. Adaptable, flexible, and accepting unless a value is threatened. Want to understand people and ways of fulfilling human potential. Little concern with possessions or surroundings.	**INTP** Quiet and reserved. Especially enjoy theoretical or scientific pursuits. Like solving problems with logic and analysis. Interested mainly in ideas, with little liking for parties or small talk. Tend to have sharply defined interests. Need careers where some strong interest can be used and useful.
Extraverts	**ESTP** Good at on-the-spot problem solving. Like action, enjoy whatever comes along. Tend to like mechanical things and sports, with friends on the side. Adaptable, tolerant, pragmatic; focused on getting results. Dislike long explanations. Are best with real things that can be worked, handled, taken apart, or put together.	**ESFP** Outgoing, accepting, friendly, enjoy everything and make things more fun for others by their enjoyment. Like action and making things happen. Know what's going on and join in eagerly. Find remembering facts easier than mastering theories. Are best in situations that need sound common sense and practical ability with people.	**ENFP** Warmly enthusiastic, high-spirited, ingenious, imaginative. Able to do almost anything that interests them. Quick with a solution or any difficulty and ready to help anyone with a problem. Often rely on their ability to improvise instead of preparing in advance. Can usually find compelling reasons for whatever they want.	**ENTP** Quick, ingenious, good at many things. Stimulating company, alert, and outspoken. May argue for fun on either side of a question. Resourceful in solving new and challenging problems, but may neglect routine assignments. Apt to turn to one new interest after another. Skillful in finding logical reasons for what they want.
	ESTJ Practical, realistic, matter-of-fact, with a natural head for business or mechanics. Not interested in abstract theories; want learning to have direct and immediate application. Like to organize and run activities. Often make good administrators; are decisive, quickly move to implement decisions; take care of routine details.	**ESFJ** Warm-hearted, talkative, popular, conscientious, born cooperators, active committee members. Need harmony and may be good at creating it. Always doing something nice for someone. Work best with encouragement and praise. Main interest is in things that directly and visibly affect people's lives.	**ENFJ** Responsive and responsible. Feel real concern for what others think or want, and try to handle things with due regard for the other's feelings. Can present a proposal or lead a group discussion with ease and tact. Sociable, popular, sympathetic. Responsive to praise and criticism. Like to facilitate others and enable people to achieve their potential.	**ENTJ** Frank, decisive. Leaders in activities. Develop and implement comprehensive systems to solve orgnizational problems. Good in anything that requires reasoning and intelligent talk, such as public speaking. Are usualy well informed and enjoy adding to their fund of knowledge.

From Introduction to Type (5th ed.), Isabel Briggs Myers. Copyright 1993 by Consulting Psychologists Press, Inc. Reproduced with permission.

■ **TABLE A-IV.2**
Characteristics Frequently Associated with Each Type

Table A-IV.3 lists just a small sampling of characteristics associated with each of the preferences, and Table A-IV.4 lists phrases that describe characteristics resulting from combinations of the preferences. Look at the resources at the back of this book for more detailed information on the MBTI and the *Strong* instruments or, as we mentioned earlier, call a career counselor.

Studying the MBTI and the *Strong* is an excellent aid to understanding who you are, a necessary component of writing a Heart & Soul resume.

Extraversion (E)
- Excellent verbal communicator
- Wide variety of skills and interests
- Strong public speaking skills
- Take initiative
- Networking skills

Introversion (I)
- Excellent written communicator
- Focused on and attentive to the problems at hand
- Highly skilled and adept within the industry
- Review alternatives thoroughly before making insightful recommendations
- Work quietly and efficiently

Sensing (S)
- Extremely resourceful
- Work well with details
- Readily identify and communicate pertinent facts of the problem at hand
- Address and manage the realities of the current situation or problem
- Build morale by appreciating and communicating the positives of the moment

Intuition (N)
- Long-term planner
- Recognize unseen business opportunities
- Vision for future possibilities
- Think of new and exciting ideas
- Apply insight to complex problem solving
- Objectively see how seemingly unrelated events and facts tie together
- Anticipate and prepare for future trends within the company and the industry
- Thrive in challenging, ever-changing environments

Thinking (T)
- Analytical, logical problem solver
- Objective, reasonable, and fair
- Strong negotiator
- Analyze consequences and implications of difficult decisions
- Identify and see flaws or problems before they happen
- Consistently maintain fair and objective policies and procedures
- Stand firm for principles that are important to the company
- Create and maintain rational, fair systems of operations

Feeling (F)
- Work well with a wide variety of people
- Excellent listener
- Create strong bonds with peers, clients, and supervisors
- Excel in a team-oriented environment
- Forecast how others will feel about new issues within the company
- Teach and coach others to be their best
- Stand firm for values that are important to the work force
- Organize people and tasks harmoniously

Judging (J)
- Organized and methodical
- Coordinate complex projects to successful closure
- Schedule and implement projects, labor hours, and systems
- Recognized for getting tasks done on time and under budget
- Maintain tight controls on operations

Perceiving (P)
- Thrive in fast-paced, competitive environments
- Adapt quickly to ever-changing environments
- Encourage feedback and new ideas from staff
- Review all options thoroughly before making decisions
- Remain flexible and open to the changes common in the workplace

■ **TABLE A-IV.3**
Type Characteristics

Phrases from Combinations of Judgment and External Preferences

Thinking and Judging (TJ)
- Tough-minded, analytical, and instrumental leader
- Make sound decisions based on principles and systems, overall impacts and rational analysis of outcomes

Feeling and Judging (FJ)
- Lead by teaching and inspiring employees
- Observant within corporate culture to create a productive and vibrant work environment

Thinking and Perceiving (TP)
- Objective and critical analysis of operations and excessive expenditures
- Structure a fair and organized system for employees to work within

Feeling and Perceiving (FP)
- Build strong working relationships within teams and various work groups
- Lead and supervise through strong employee support, coaching, and encouragement

Phrases from Combinations of Judgment and Perception Preferences

Sensing and Thinking (ST)
- Results- and bottom-line–oriented

Intuition and Thinking (NT)
- Thrive on opportunities for problem solving, analysis, and design

Sensing and Feeling (SF)
- Drawn to opportunities for practical service to people

Intuition and Feeling (NF)
- Recognize and help people reach their full potential

Phrases from Combinations of Direction of Energy and External Orientation

Introversion and Judging (IJ)
- Persevere through challenging tasks and assignments
- Develop organized, well–thought-out systems

Extraversion and Judging (EJ)
- Lead and work quickly and confidently
- Recognized for getting things done!

Introversion and Perceiving (IP)
- Extremely flexible within daily operations
- Believe in and work toward sound principles set within the company

Extraversion and Perceiving (EP)
- Thrive in a fast-paced, ever-changing environment
- Readily accept and enjoy new challenges

Adapted from Introduction to Type *(5th ed.), Isabel Briggs Myers. Copyright 1993 by Consulting Psychologists Press. Reprinted with permission.*

■ **TABLE A-IV.4**
Phrases from Combinations of Preferences

A Brief History of the Strong Interest Inventory (Strong)

The idea of measuring people's interests has been around since World War I, when military psychologists wrestled with the problem of how to determine which recruits should be cooks and which should be members of the cavalry. Most of us recognize that the type of person who likes the job of cooking is different from the type of person who likes the job of riding and tending horses, and the idea of classifying people by their interests has some intuitive appeal. After World War I, it became clear to some of those same psychologists that the idea had important implications for civilians as well. If it were possible to measure people's vocational interests and to use those data along with information about abilities and values, it might be possible to perform two important interrelated services. First, individuals could be helped in making educational and career plans. Second, the common interests of people working in various occupations could be described. These ideas led to the development of the *Strong Interest Inventory.*

The *Strong* compares a person's responses to various questions regarding career interests to the patterns of responses of people of different personality types and in different occupations. This combination of information allows assumptions to be made about whether an individual is likely to find satisfaction in the work typically done in a given occupation.

The *Strong* gives the respondent five main types of information: first, scores on 6 General Occupational Themes (see Figure A-IV.1, page 172), which reflect the respondent's overall orientation to work; second, scores on 25 Basic Interest Scales, which report consistency of interests or aversions in 25 specific areas, such as art, science, and public speaking; third, scores on 211 Occupational Scales representing 109 different occupations, which indicate the degree of similarity between the respondent's interests and the characteristic interests of women and men working in those occupations; fourth, scores on 4 Personal Style Scales, which measure aspects of the style with which an individual likes to learn, work, assume leadership, and take risks; and fifth, 3 types of Administrative Indexes, which help identify invalid or unusual profiles for special attention.

Common Phrases Associated with Each General Occupational Theme

Table A-IV.5 (page 173) presents phrases commonly associated with the General Occupational Themes (GOTs) found in the *Strong Interest Inventory.* These descriptive phrases can help a person understand why he or she likes certain work environments more than others and responds better to certain types of work situations than others. The results of the *Strong Interest Inventory* can be extremely valuable in helping you get to the heart and soul of your career dreams. Look at the phrases we've listed. Which ones best describe you? What examples can you think of to support each phrase?

General Occupational Themes

The six General Occupational Themes describe vocational or career interests, as well as occupations and working environments. The following chart provides you with examples of interests, activities, skills, and values of people who fall into each of the six Themes. These examples, however, are generalizations; none will fit any one person exactly. In fact, most people's interests combine several Themes to some degree. Although some people do not indicate interests in any of the Themes, or in only one of them, most show an average or a high degree of interest in two or three of them. In career planning, try to identify occupations whose typical activities combine the interests suggested by your General Occupational Theme scores.

These six themes can be arranged around a hexagon with the types most similar to each other falling next to each other, and those

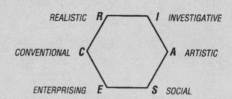

most dissimilar falling directly across the hexagon from one another. For example, as shown in the hexagon above, the Realistic and Investigative Themes are next to each other. People of these two types show some similarity—they generally like to solve technical problems and to work alone. On the other hand, the Realistic and Social Themes are opposite one another on the hexagon. Therefore, people of these two types usually have dissimilar interests. For example, unlike the Realistic types who like working through problems on their own, the Social types like to solve problems by discussing them with others in groups.

THEME	INTERESTS	WORK ACTIVITIES	POTENTIAL SKILLS	VALUES
Realistic (R)	Machines, tools, outdoors	Operating equipment, using tools, building, repairing	Mechanical ingenuity and dexterity, physical coordination	Tradition, practicality, common sense
Investigative (I)	Science, theories, ideas, data	Performing lab work, solving abstract problems, researching	Math, writing, analysis	Independence, curiosity, learning
Artistic (A)	Self-expression, art appreciation	Composing music, writing, creating visual art	Creativity, musical talent, artistic expression	Beauty, originality, independence, imagination
Social (S)	People, team work, human welfare, community service	Teaching, explaining, helping	People skills, verbal ability, listening, showing understanding	Cooperation, generosity, service to others
Enterprising (E)	Business, politics, leadership, influence	Selling, managing, persuading	Verbal ability, ability to motivate and direct others	Risk taking, status, competition
Conventional (C)	Organization, data, finance	Setting up procedures, organizing, operating computers	Math, data analysis, record keeping, attention to detail	Accuracy, stability, efficiency

From Strong Interest Inventory: Applications and Technical Guide, *Lenore W. Harmon, Jo-Ida Hansen, Fred H. Borgen, Allen L. Hammer. Copyright 1993 by Consulting Psychologists Press. Reproduced with permission.*

■ **FIGURE A-IV.1**
General Occupational Themes (GOTs)

The Realistic Type
- Concrete problem solver
- Stable, dedicated, and hardworking employee
- Thrive in new, challenging environments
- Lead by example
- Work independently
- Take initiative with little or no supervision
- Set and achieve clear, measurable goals and deadlines
- Strong physical and motor skills
- Appreciate traditional systems and corporate cultures
- Excellent project manager

The Investigative Type
- Solve highly complex and intellectual problems
- Work well independently and autonomously
- Create and design solutions to problems
- Insightful and analytical problem solver
- Take initiative
- Strategic planner with strong analytical skills
- Develop and nurture an intellectually stimulating environment
- Constantly striving for a better way of doing things
- Motivate intellectual achievement
- Monitor progress on goals

The Artistic Type
- Develop inventive and creative projects
- Inspired by new, challenging projects
- Remain flexible in fast-paced, ever-changing environment
- Skilled at bringing new ideas to the table when called upon
- Encourage staff to work independently, with minimal supervision
- Excellent communicator
- Excited and enthusiastic about products and services
- Imaginative and observant
- Create new and exciting systems and designs

The Social Type
- Build motivated work environment
- Improve productivity by listening and helping employees work through problems
- Maintain the highest professional, ethical, and service standards
- Work extremely hard
- "Hands-on" leader, willing to work at all levels to get the job done
- Skilled at positioning staff where they will be most productive
- Strong team player
- Excellent at appeasing customers and employees in stressful or trying situations
- Maintain willingness and desire to help others
- Friendly, cheerful, and warm

■ **TABLE A-IV.5**
Common Phrases Associated with Each General Occupational Theme

The Enterprising Type
- Proven marketing and sales skills
- Strong negotiator
- Thrive in a challenging, competitive environment
- Excellent leadership skills
- Sell and promote ideas
- Possess a dynamic, outgoing, and energetic style
- Work diligently to get the most out of others
- Provide direction and leadership to company
- Excel in competitive, highly visible positions
- Comfortably take charge when called upon

The Conventional Type
- Conscientious, responsible, and reliable
- Run operations and procedures according to plan
- Build and maintain consistent methodology and systems
- Proven ability to organize complex systems
- Excellent with details, providing clear, explicit instructions
- Lead and supervise with clear goals and work well in a team environment
- Utilize strong experience base to carefully and completely train staff
- Clearly write and implement policies and procedures
- Emphasize efficiency and accuracy within department
- Excellent numerical, computing, and organizational skills
- Work well with company leadership, follow and adhere to lines of authority

Adapted from Strong Interest Inventory: Applications and Technical Guide, *Lenore W. Harmon, Jo-Ida Hansen, Fred H. Borgen, Allen L. Hammer. Copyright 1993 by Consulting Psychologists Press. Reproduced with permission.*

■ **TABLE A-IV.5 CONTINUED**
Common Phrases Associated with Each General Occupational Theme

About the Authors

CHUCK COCHRAN

Chuck Cochran formally started his company ResumePLUS, Inc., also known as The Heart & Soul Career Center, in 1991 and has since helped thousands of executives, professionals, and young people with all aspects of their job search and career development. He cofounded the *Heart & Soul* career book series concept, which implements a more insightful psychological approach to helping individuals pursue their dreams.

He knows goals are never achieved by accident, and therefore teaches the need for creating a personal mission and objectives that will guide your career and life to wherever you want to be, both professionally and personally. He knows that your success in the job market as well as other endeavors depends on your commitment and focus. Chuck also works with organizations and businesses in teaching this very important message, which is key in team building, communication, and organizational development. He is an experienced career professional and actively utilizes the *Myers-Briggs Type Indicator* and *Strong Interest Inventory* in his work.

As a respected speaker, Chuck uses a warm and entertaining way of putting his audience at ease and lays a foundation of knowledge and trust that allows the participants to openly discuss and plan life issues that affect them every day. Whether the setting is a seminar, workshop, meeting, convention, or non-profit event, participants always walk away with life and career changing tools they can implement immediately. Chuck speaks nationally on topics of success, life planning, career development, job searching, resume writing, team building, communication, and organizational development.

While his interests and passions are as wide as they are varied, his time is equally split between his family and his business. As an avid outdoorsman, Chuck is a huge fan of basketball, golf, tennis, and SEC football. He writes music, plays guitar, and loves being near the music industry in Nashville. He lives with his wife, Michelle, his son, Dean, and his two dogs, Eddie and Emma, and can be reached at the Heart & Soul Career Center.

DONNA PEERCE

Donna Peerce began her professional writing career in elementary school when she published her first short story in a newspaper. This inspired her to continue in her writing endeavors and to combine these with art, broadcast production, and business communications. Throughout her life, she has always implemented a Heart & Soul approach to her writing and to her everyday experiences.

While attending Western Kentucky University in Bowling Green, Donna won several literary awards for short stories, essays, and poetry. After graduating with a bachelor of arts degree in radio, television, and journalism, she worked for commercial and public television studios, honing her skills as a producer/director and scriptwriter. Combining her video production skills with writing was a natural for her, and she continues to freelance as a broadcast producer, director, and writer. As an international workshop presenter, Donna travels throughout the United States and Canada to facilitate Heart & Soul writing workshops.

With more than 15 years of experience as a professional writer, Donna has worked for national advertising agencies and is a ghostwriter of six published novels. An accomplished artist, her work has been published by Hallmark, American Greetings, and Gibson Greeting Cards. Donna's hobbies include aerobics, spinning, the Internet, reading, art, hiking in the woods, writing songs for fun, singing, and travel.

Donna is a world traveler and has roamed the quaint villages of Europe in search of her true destiny. After numerous years of travel, dream study, and spiritual study, Donna firmly believes that life is a spiritual experience and that the real search for the meaning of life begins within yourself. Therein lies all answers. Her professional goal is to teach people how to put heart and soul into their lives and discover their own inner answers, and to help them find the job of their dreams!

Born in Kentucky, the eldest of eight siblings, Donna now resides in Nashville, Tennessee. She began writing resumes to supplement her income in 1988 and, in 1993, joined Chuck Cochran at ResumePLUS, Inc./Heart & Soul Career Center, where she is vice president of Writing Services. She cofounded the *Heart & Soul* career book series concept, which implements a more insightful psychological approach to helping individuals pursue their dreams. She is currently a member of the National Career Development Association and has assisted thousands of individuals in discovering and reaching for their dreams.

Donna is continuously working on Heart & Soul writing projects and looks forward to sharing more stories with Heart & Soul readers in the future!

HOW TO REACH THE AUTHORS

We would love to hear your stories. Please write, e-mail, or call! If you are having trouble with your resume, we would be glad to critique it for you. Contact us for our availability on speaking and consulting.

OUR WEB PAGE	www.mindspring.com/~heartsoul
E-MAIL	Chuck Cochran: heartsoul@mindspring.com
	Donna Peerce: dpeerce@mindspring.com
OUR ADDRESS	The Heart & Soul Career Center
	ResumePLUS, Inc.
	1808 West End, Suite 1012
	Nashville, TN 37203
	(615) 329-0300
OR CONTACT	Davies-Black Publishing
	An Imprint of Consulting Psychologists Press, Inc.
	3803 East Bayshore Road
	Palo Alto, CA 94303
	www.cpp-db.com

HEART & SOUL TIP

Check out our Web site for the latest information on our books, services, and company.

Acknowledgments

As always, I want to thank my family—my parents and my brothers and sisters (and their spouses) for their wonderful support and encouragement. All seven of my brothers and sisters—Vickie, Allan, Greg, Karen, Bart, Marla, and Philip (as well as their spouses, Paul, Steve, Debbie, Yvonda, and Marcia)—are great friends and wonderful people to know. I thank my nephews and nieces for their love: Chad, Bryce, Joshua, Jason, Matthew, Reece, Tyler, Dustin, Ally, and Bethany. My family has taught me about love and the true values of life.

In addition, I will always be grateful for my best friend, Jackie, who is forever willing to give of herself and her heart to me at any time, day or night, during moments of stress, heartache, pain, joy, and laughter. I also thank her husband, Bob, and their two daughters, Sunny and Amber, for sharing their mom with me!

I thank my other special friends, Annie, Aldie, Michael, Judith, Amy, Wanda, and others for their friendship and support.

I thank Chuck for being my partner through the writing of these Heart & Soul books and for the great opportunities that have come my way.

Of course, I thank Melinda Adams Merino, Laura Simonds, and Lee Langhammer Law at Davies-Black Publishing for their ongoing support and vision for the Heart & Soul series of books. It is a joy knowing them and working with them.

I thank all the people who have endorsed our Heart & Soul books. These authors have clearly shared our vision for the books and are true inspirations themselves!

Last, but certainly not least, I thank my spiritual guide and mentor, Harold, who has shown me the way to spiritual freedom. Without his guidance I would still be just a child in the wilderness wandering aimlessly in search of myself.

DONNA PEERCE

To my son, Dean, born July 10, 1998, the only person in the world who could wake my wife and me up every two hours, demanding food and attention, and still melt our hearts with those *"I'm so cute, you will do whatever I say"* eyes. You're my little man!

Endearing thanks to Donna Peerce, Melinda Adams Merino, Laura Simonds, and Lee Langhammer Law for their support, enthusiasm, and never-ending energy!

CHUCK COCHRAN

Index